COMPLETE INSTAGRAM MARKETING SECRETS

The guide and strategies on how to market your product, find customer and grow your business

Kane Schiller

Copyright

Table of Contents

Introduction

In a bustling city filled with aspiring entrepreneurs and ambitious dreamers, there lived a young man named Michael. Michael had a passion for fashion and had recently launched his own online boutique, selling handmade jewelry and accessories. He poured his heart and soul into creating unique pieces, but despite his efforts, he struggled to attract customers to his store.

Day after day, Michael would anxiously check his website traffic and social media metrics, hoping for a spike in engagement or a surge in sales. However, his efforts seemed to go unnoticed, and her inbox remained eerily empty, devoid of any customer inquiries or orders.

Feeling disheartened and frustrated, Michael began to question whether his dream of running a successful business was just that—a dream. He wondered if he had made a mistake by venturing into the world of entrepreneurship, and he contemplated giving up altogether.

One day, while browsing the shelves of his local bookstore in search of inspiration, Michael stumbled upon a book titled **"COMPLETE INSTAGRAM MARKETING SECRETS:** The guide and strategies on how to market your product, find customers and grow your business." Intrigued by the promise of unlocking the secrets to Instagram success, Michael decided to purchase the book and give it a read.

As he delved into the pages of the book, Michael was captivated by the wealth of knowledge and practical advice it contained. He learned about the importance of optimizing his Instagram profile, crafting compelling content, and engaging with his audience authentically. He discovered strategies for using hashtags effectively, collaborating with influencers, and leveraging Instagram's advertising platform to reach her target market.

Armed with newfound knowledge and a renewed sense of purpose, Michael set out to implement the strategies outlined in the book. He revamped his

Instagram profile, curated stunning visuals of his jewelry collections, and started engaging with his audience by sharing behind-the-scenes glimpses of his creative process.

To her surprise and delight, Michael began to see results almost immediately. His follower count started to climb, and his posts garnered likes, comments, and shares from eager fans and potential customers. Before long, orders began pouring in, and Michael's once-empty inbox was now overflowing with inquiries and messages from excited shoppers.

With each passing day, Michael's online boutique flourished, thanks to the invaluable lessons he had learned from the book. He was no longer a struggling entrepreneur but a confident businessman who had unlocked the secrets to Instagram marketing success.

And so, with determination, perseverance, and a little help from a book titled **"COMPLETE INSTAGRAM MARKETING SECRETS,"** Michael's dream of building a thriving business became a reality, proving that with the right knowledge and strategy, anything is possible.

Introduction

Welcome to Instagram Marketing

Welcome to **"COMPLETE INSTAGRAM MARKETING SECRETS"**! Whether you're a novice looking to dip your toes into the world of social media marketing or a seasoned marketer aiming to refine your strategies, this book is designed to be your comprehensive guide. Instagram, with over a billion active users, has emerged as one of the most powerful platforms for businesses of all sizes. Its visually driven interface, coupled with robust engagement tools, provides a unique opportunity to connect with your audience in a meaningful way.

In this book, we will unlock the secrets to mastering Instagram marketing. You will learn how to craft captivating content, build and engage a loyal audience, and ultimately drive sales and grow your business. The journey to Instagram success begins here, and we're excited to guide you every step of the way.

The Importance of Instagram for Your Business

Why Instagram? The answer lies in its unparalleled ability to engage users through visual storytelling. Unlike other social media platforms, Instagram thrives on aesthetics and creativity, making it an ideal space for businesses to showcase their products and services. With features like Stories, Reels, and IGTV, Instagram offers various ways to connect with potential customers, each catering to different aspects of user engagement.

In today's digital age, having a strong Instagram presence is not just beneficial—it's essential. A well-executed Instagram strategy can help you:
- **Build Brand Awareness:** Reach a global audience and make your brand recognizable.
- **Engage with Customers:** Foster relationships through direct interactions and personalized content.

- Drive Traffic and Sales: Utilize Instagram's shopping features and targeted ads to convert followers into customers.

- Gain Insights: Leverage Instagram's analytics to understand your audience and refine your marketing efforts.

By mastering Instagram marketing, you position your business to thrive in an increasingly competitive online marketplace.

How to Use This Book

This book is structured to provide a step-by-step guide to mastering Instagram marketing. Each chapter builds upon the previous one, ensuring a cohesive learning experience that covers the fundamentals and advanced strategies alike. Here's how to make the most of this book:

1. Start with the Basics: If you're new to Instagram or social media marketing, begin with Chapter 1 to establish a solid foundation. This chapter covers everything from setting up your business profile to defining your brand's voice.

2. Dive into Content Creation: Chapter 2 is dedicated to helping you create compelling content that resonates with your audience. Learn the art of crafting posts, Stories, and Reels that captivate and engage.

3. Focus on Audience Engagement: In Chapter 3, discover strategies for growing and interacting with your audience. Building a loyal follower base and fostering engagement are crucial for long-term success.

4. Implement Advanced Strategies: Chapter 4 delves into advanced marketing techniques, including advertising, influencer partnerships, and analytics. These strategies will help you optimize your efforts and achieve better results.

5. Monetize Your Efforts: Chapter 5 guides you through the process of turning your Instagram presence into a revenue-generating machine. From seamless shopping experiences to customer retention, this chapter covers it all.

6. Utilize the Appendices: The appendix section provides additional resources, including a glossary of Instagram terms, recommended tools, and templates to streamline your marketing efforts.

7. Reflect and Recap: The conclusion offers a summary of key takeaways and looks at the future of Instagram marketing, encouraging you to continue evolving your strategies.

By following this structure, you'll gain a comprehensive understanding of Instagram marketing and be equipped with the tools and knowledge needed to succeed. Let's get started on your journey to Instagram mastery!

Chapter 1: Laying the Foundation

Understanding Instagram Basics

Before diving into advanced strategies, it's essential to grasp the fundamentals of Instagram. As a visually-driven platform, Instagram thrives on compelling imagery and videos. Unlike other social media networks, Instagram emphasizes aesthetics and storytelling through visual content, making it crucial to understand its unique features and functionalities.

The Instagram Interface

Familiarize yourself with the main components of Instagram:

1. Profile: Your business profile is your brand's face on Instagram. It includes your profile picture, bio, posts, stories, and more.

2. Feed: The feed is where you see posts from accounts you follow. It's the primary area for users to interact with your content.

3. Explore: The Explore page helps users discover new content and accounts based on their interests and engagement patterns.

4. Stories: Instagram Stories are temporary posts that last for 24 hours, perfect for sharing behind-the-scenes content and real-time updates.

5. Reels: Short, engaging videos that can go viral, Reels are ideal for reaching new audiences.

6. IGTV: IGTV allows for longer videos, making it suitable for more in-depth content and series.

7. Direct Messages (DMs): This feature enables private conversations with your followers, facilitating customer service and engagement.

Setting Up Your Business Profile

Your business profile on Instagram is the first impression potential customers have of your brand. It's crucial to set it up correctly to ensure it reflects your brand identity and conveys your value proposition clearly.

Profile Picture

Choose a profile picture that represents your brand effectively. This could be your logo or a professional image that aligns with your brand identity. Ensure the image is clear and recognizable even in a small, circular format.

Bio

Your bio is a 150-character summary of your business. It should be concise, informative, and engaging. Include essential information such as:

- What your business does
- Your unique selling proposition (USP)
- A call to action (e.g., "Shop now," "Follow us for updates")
- A link to your website or a specific landing page

Contact Information

Make it easy for followers to reach you by adding contact options like an email address, phone number, and physical address if applicable. Instagram allows you to include buttons for direct contact via email, phone, or message.

Business Category

Select a category that accurately represents your business. This helps users understand what your business is about at a glance.

Defining Your Brand's Voice and Aesthetic

Consistency is key on Instagram. Your brand's voice and aesthetic should be coherent across all posts to create a cohesive and recognizable presence.

Brand Voice

Determine the tone and style of your communication. Are you formal or casual? Friendly or authoritative? Your brand voice should align with your target audience and overall brand personality.

Visual Aesthetic

Choose a visual theme that reflects your brand identity. This includes:

- **Color Scheme:** Use a consistent color palette in your posts. This helps in creating a uniform look and feel.
- **Filters and Editing Style:** Stick to a particular set of filters and editing techniques to maintain visual consistency.
- **Content Themes:** Identify the main types of content you will post (e.g., product photos, behind-the-scenes shots, user-generated content).

Setting SMART Goals for Your Instagram Strategy

To succeed on Instagram, you need clear, actionable goals. The SMART framework (Specific,

Measurable, Achievable, Relevant, Time-bound) helps in setting effective objectives.

Specific

Your goals should be precise and clear. Instead of saying "increase followers," specify "increase followers by 20%."

Measurable

Ensure your goals can be quantified. This allows you to track progress and measure success. For instance, "gain 500 new followers" or "achieve a 10% engagement rate."

Achievable

Set realistic goals based on your current situation and resources. While ambitious goals are great, they should still be attainable.

Relevant

Your goals should align with your overall business objectives. For example, if your primary aim is to drive sales, focus on goals like "increase website traffic through Instagram by 30%."

Time-bound

Set deadlines for your goals to create a sense of urgency and keep you on track. For example, "gain 500 new followers in three months."

Example SMART Goals

- Increase Instagram followers by 20% within six months.
- Achieve a 10% engagement rate on posts over the next quarter.
- Drive a 30% increase in website traffic from Instagram within three months.
- Generate 50 new leads through Instagram Stories in the next two months.

By laying a strong foundation, you set the stage for successful Instagram marketing. With a well-crafted profile, a clear brand identity, and SMART goals, you're ready to move on to creating compelling content and building a loyal audience.

Setting Up a Business Profile

Your business profile on Instagram is the first impression potential customers have of your brand. It's crucial to set it up correctly to ensure it reflects your brand identity and conveys your value proposition clearly.

Profile Picture

Choose a profile picture that represents your brand effectively. This could be your logo or a professional image that aligns with your brand identity. Ensure the image is clear and recognizable even in a small, circular format.

Bio

Your bio is a 150-character summary of your business. It should be concise, informative, and engaging. Include essential information such as:

- What your business does
- Your unique selling proposition (USP)
- A call to action (e.g., "Shop now," "Follow us for updates")
- A link to your website or a specific landing page

Contact Information

Make it easy for followers to reach you by adding contact options like an email address, phone number, and physical address if applicable. Instagram allows you to include buttons for direct contact via email, phone, or message.

Business Category

Select a category that accurately represents your business. This helps users understand what your business is about at a glance.

Action Buttons

Instagram offers several action buttons that can be added to your profile to facilitate direct interactions with your audience. These buttons include:

- **Email:** Allows users to send you an email directly from your profile.
- **Call:** Provides users with a one-click option to call your business.
- **Directions:** Offers a map and directions to your physical location.
- **Book:** Enables users to book appointments directly from your profile through integrated third-party partners.

Instagram Shopping

If you sell products, setting up Instagram Shopping is a must. It allows you to tag products in your posts and stories, enabling users to shop directly from your profile.

To set up Instagram Shopping, you need to:

1. Create a Facebook Shop: Your Instagram Shop is linked to your Facebook Shop, so you must have one set up.

2. Add a Product Catalog: Upload your products to the Facebook Shop to create a catalog.

3. Sign Up for Instagram Shopping: Apply for Instagram Shopping through your business profile settings.

Profile Optimization Tips

1. Consistency: Use a consistent username across all social media platforms to make it easy for users to find you.

2. Keywords: Incorporate relevant keywords into your bio to enhance discoverability.

3. Hashtags: Consider adding branded hashtags in your bio to encourage user-generated content.

4. Highlights: Use Instagram Highlights to showcase important content, such as product launches, customer testimonials, and behind-the-scenes footage.

Example of an Effective Business Profile

Profile Picture

A clean and simple logo that is easily recognizable.

Bio

"Eco-friendly fashion for the conscious consumer | Sustainable materials, ethical production | Worldwide shipping | Shop now: [link]"

Contact Information

- **Email:** contact@yourbrand.com
- **Call:** +1-234-567-890
- **Address:** 123 Green Street, Eco City, EC 12345

Business Category

Fashion & Apparel

Action Buttons

- Email
- Call
- Directions
- **Book** (if applicable)

Highlights

- **New Arrivals**
- **Best Sellers**
- **Customer Reviews**
- **Sustainability**

By setting up a professional and engaging business profile, you establish a strong foundation for your Instagram marketing efforts. This optimized profile not only attracts potential customers but also encourages them to engage with your brand, leading to higher conversion rates and increased brand loyalty.

Defining Your Brand and Audience

To create an effective Instagram marketing strategy, it's crucial to have a clear understanding of your brand and target audience. Defining these elements ensures that your content resonates with the right people and consistently conveys your brand's message and values.

Understanding Your Brand

Your brand is more than just your logo or tagline; it encompasses your business's identity, values, and the promise you make to your customers.

How to define your brand effectively:

Brand Identity

1. Mission Statement: What is the primary goal of your business? What do you aim to achieve for your customers and the world at large?

2. Core Values: What principles guide your business decisions? These could include sustainability, innovation, customer-centricity, etc.

3. Unique Selling Proposition (USP): What makes your brand stand out from the competition? Identify the unique benefits or features that you offer.

Brand Personality

1. Voice and Tone: How do you communicate with your audience? Are you formal, casual, friendly, authoritative, witty, or serious?

2. Visual Style: What visual elements represent your brand? This includes your color palette, typography, and overall aesthetic.

Brand Story

1. Origin: How did your brand come to be? Share the story behind your business's inception.

2. Journey: What milestones and challenges have you overcome? This narrative can create a deeper connection with your audience.

Identifying Your Target Audience

Knowing your audience is essential to tailoring your content, messaging, and marketing efforts. Here's how to identify and understand your target audience:

Demographics

1. Age: What age group does your target audience belong to?

2. Gender: Is your audience predominantly male, female, or a mix of both?

3. Location: Where are your target customers located? Are they local, national, or international?

4. Income Level: What is the average income of your target audience?

5. Education Level: What is the education level of your audience?

Psychographics

1. Interests: What are the hobbies and interests of your target audience?

2. Values and Beliefs: What values and beliefs do they hold? This can help in aligning your brand messaging with their ideals.

3. Lifestyle: What does a day in the life of your target customer look like? Understanding their daily activities can help tailor your content to their routine.

Behavioral Aspects

1. Buying Behavior: How does your audience typically make purchasing decisions? Are they impulsive buyers or do they conduct thorough research?

2. Pain Points: What challenges and problems do they face that your product or service can solve?

3. Engagement: How does your audience interact with brands on Instagram? Do they prefer stories, posts, reels, or direct messages?

Creating Audience Personas

Develop detailed audience personas to visualize and understand your target customers better. Each persona should include:

- **Name and Photo:** Give your persona a name and a representative photo to make them feel real.
- **Demographic Information:** Age, gender, location, occupation, income level, etc.
- **Psychographic Information:** Interests, values, lifestyle, and behavior.
- **Goals and Challenges:** What are their main objectives and what obstacles do they face?
- **Preferred Social Media Channels:** Where do they spend most of their time online?

Example Audience Persona

Persona Name: Eco-conscious Emma

- **Age:** 28
- **Gender:** Female
- **Location:** San Francisco, CA
- **Occupation:** Graphic Designer
- **Income Level:** $55,000/year

- **Education Level:** Bachelor's Degree
- **Interests:** Sustainable living, vegan cooking, yoga, travel
- **Values and Beliefs:** Environmental sustainability, ethical consumerism, minimalism
- **Lifestyle:** Lives in a small apartment, commutes by bike, prefers shopping at local and organic stores
- **Goals and Challenges:** Aims to reduce her carbon footprint, struggles to find affordable, sustainable products
- **Preferred Social Media Channels:** Instagram and Pinterest

By defining your brand and understanding your audience, you can create more relevant and engaging content that appeals to your target customers. This clarity will guide your overall Instagram strategy, helping you connect with the right people and build a loyal community around your brand.

Crafting a Winning Bio and Profile

Your Instagram bio and profile are your brand's first impression. They need to capture your audience's attention, convey your brand identity, and encourage engagement. Here's how to craft a compelling bio and optimize your profile for success.

Writing a Captivating Bio

Your Instagram bio is limited to 150 characters, so every word counts. It should succinctly communicate who you are, what you do, and why people should follow you.

Here's a step-by-step guide:

1. Clear and Concise Description:
   - **Who You Are:** Start with your brand name or a brief description of what your business does.

- What You Offer: Highlight your unique selling proposition (USP). What makes your brand special or different from others?

- Why Follow: Give a reason for people to follow you. This could be the type of content you share, the value you provide, or a specific call to action.

2. Include Keywords:

- Use relevant keywords that potential followers might use when searching for brands like yours. This enhances your discoverability on Instagram.

3. Emojis:

- Incorporate emojis to break up text, add personality, and make your bio visually appealing. Use them to highlight key points or guide users' eyes to important information.

4. Call to Action (CTA):

- Include a strong CTA that directs visitors to take a specific action, such as visiting your website, shopping your products, or following your account.

5. Link:

- Use the link in your bio to direct followers to your website, a specific landing page, or a Linktree (a tool that allows you to share multiple links).

Bio Examples

Example 1: E-commerce Store
Bio: Eco-friendly fashion for the conscious consumer | Sustainable materials | Worldwide shipping | Shop now: [link]

Example 2: Fitness Coach
Bio: Helping you achieve your fitness goals | Personalized workout plans & nutrition tips | Join the #FitFam | Start today: [link]

Optimizing Your Profile

A well-optimized profile enhances your brand's credibility and encourages interaction.

How to set up your profile for success:

1. Profile Picture:

- Choose a profile picture that represents your brand, such as your logo or a professional headshot. Ensure it is clear and recognizable even in a small, circular format.

2. Username:

- Use a username that is consistent with your brand name and other social media handles. This makes it easier for users to find you.

3. Display Name:

- Your display name can include your brand name and a keyword to increase discoverability. For example, "EcoFashion - Sustainable Clothing."

4. Category:

- Select a category that accurately describes your business. This helps users understand what your business is about at a glance.

5. Contact Information:

- Include options for users to contact you directly. Add an email address, phone number, and physical address if applicable. Instagram allows you to add contact buttons for easy access.

6. Story Highlights:

- Use Story Highlights to keep important stories accessible on your profile. Organize them into categories such as "New Arrivals," "Customer Reviews," "Behind the Scenes," or "Tutorials."

Example Profile Optimization

Profile Picture

- A clean and recognizable logo of your brand.

Username

- @EcoFashionStore

Display Name

- EcoFashion - Sustainable Clothing

Bio

- Eco-friendly fashion for the conscious consumer | Sustainable materials | Worldwide shipping | Shop now: [link]

Category

- Fashion & Apparel

Contact Information

- Email: contact@ecofashionstore.com
- Call: +1-234-567-890
- Address: 123 Green Street, Eco City, EC 12345

Story Highlights

- **New Arrivals**
- **Best Sellers**
- **Customer Reviews**
- **Sustainability**
- **Behind the Scenes**

By crafting a captivating bio and optimizing your profile, you create a strong, cohesive brand presence on Instagram. This not only attracts potential followers but also encourages them to engage with your content and take action, ultimately driving growth and success for your business.

Chapter 2: Content Creation Mastery

Creating engaging, high-quality content is the cornerstone of a successful Instagram marketing strategy. This chapter delves into the essential aspects of content creation, from developing a robust content plan to utilizing Instagram's various features to captivate and grow your audience.

Developing a Content Plan

A well-crafted content plan ensures consistency, aligns your posts with your overall marketing goals, and helps you stay organized.

How to develop an effective content plan:

Define Your Content Goals

Start by identifying what you aim to achieve with your Instagram content. Clear goals will guide the type of content you produce and how you measure success. Common content goals include:

- **Brand Awareness:** Increasing visibility and recognition of your brand.
- **Engagement:** Encouraging likes, comments, shares, and saves.
- **Traffic:** Driving visitors to your website or landing pages.
- **Conversions:** Turning followers into customers.
- **Customer Loyalty:** Building a community of repeat customers and brand advocates.

Content Themes and Pillars

Establishing content themes and pillars helps maintain variety while ensuring your content remains cohesive and aligned with your brand identity. Consider these common content themes:

- **Educational:** Tutorials, tips, and how-to guides related to your industry.
- **Inspirational:** Quotes, success stories, and aspirational posts that resonate with your audience's values and aspirations.

- Promotional: Posts highlighting products, special offers, and sales.

- Behind-the-Scenes: Showcasing the human side of your brand, such as team activities, production processes, and company culture.

- User-Generated Content: Sharing content created by your customers or followers to build community and trust.

Content Calendar

A content calendar helps you plan and organize your posts in advance. This ensures consistency and allows you to align your content with key dates, events, and campaigns. When creating your content calendar, consider the following:

- Frequency: Determine how often you will post (e.g., daily, bi-weekly).

- Timing: Identify the best times to post based on when your audience is most active.

- Content Mix: Balance different types of content to keep your feed diverse and engaging.

Creating High-Quality Visual Content

Instagram is a visual platform, so the quality of your images and videos is paramount. Here's how to create visually appealing content that stands out:

Photography Tips

1. Lighting: Good lighting is essential for high-quality photos. Natural light is often the best, so try to shoot during the day. If you're shooting indoors, use soft, diffused lighting to avoid harsh shadows.

2. Composition: Follow basic composition principles such as the rule of thirds to create balanced and aesthetically pleasing images.

3. Background: Use clean, uncluttered backgrounds to make your subject stand out. For product photos, consider using props that complement your product without overpowering it.

4. Consistency: Maintain a consistent visual style across your posts. This could involve using the same filters, color schemes, and editing techniques.

Video Content

1. Short and Engaging: Keep your videos concise and to the point. Instagram Stories and Reels are particularly effective for short, engaging content.

2. High Resolution: Ensure your videos are high resolution to maintain a professional look.

3. Captions and Subtitles: Many users watch videos without sound, so adding captions or subtitles can enhance engagement and accessibility.

4. Storytelling: Use video to tell compelling stories about your brand, products, or customers. This helps build an emotional connection with your audience.

Leveraging Instagram Features

Instagram offers various features that can enhance your content and engage your audience:

Posts

- **Single Image/Video Posts:** Great for detailed shots and specific messages.
- **Carousel Posts:** Allow you to share multiple images or videos in a single post, ideal for tutorials, step-by-step guides, and showcasing product variations.

Stories

- **Ephemeral Content:** Stories disappear after 24 hours, making them perfect for behind-the-scenes content, limited-time offers, and real-time updates.
- **Interactive Elements:** Use polls, quizzes, and question stickers to engage your audience and encourage interaction.
- **Highlights:** Save your best stories in Highlights to keep them accessible on your profile.

Reels

- **Short-Form Video:** Reels are ideal for creating fun, engaging, and shareable content. Use trends, music, and creative editing to capture attention.

- Discoverability: Reels can be discovered by a wider audience through the Reels tab, making them a powerful tool for increasing reach.

IGTV

- Long-Form Content: IGTV allows you to share longer videos, perfect for in-depth tutorials, interviews, and series.
- Series: Create a series of related videos to keep your audience coming back for more.

Engaging Captions and Hashtags

Crafting Captions

1. Voice and Tone: Write captions that reflect your brand's voice and personality. Whether you're formal, casual, witty, or inspirational, consistency is key.
2. Storytelling: Use captions to tell a story, provide context, or share behind-the-scenes insights.
3. Calls to Action: Encourage engagement by including clear calls to action, such as asking

questions, prompting followers to share their thoughts, or directing them to your bio link.

4. Length: While Instagram allows up to 2,200 characters, focus on making your captions concise and impactful. The first sentence should grab attention, as it's what appears in the feed preview.

Using Hashtags

1. Relevance: Use hashtags that are relevant to your content and industry. This helps attract the right audience.

2. Mix of Popular and Niche: Combine popular hashtags with niche ones to increase visibility while targeting a specific audience.

3. Branded Hashtags: Create a unique hashtag for your brand to encourage user-generated content and community building.

4. Number of Hashtags: Instagram allows up to 30 hashtags per post, but the optimal number is typically between 5 and 11 for balanced reach and engagement.

Monitoring and Adapting

Analytics

Regularly monitor your Instagram analytics to understand what content resonates with your audience and meets your goals. Key metrics to track include:

- **Engagement Rate:** Likes, comments, shares, and saves.
- **Reach and Impressions:** The number of unique users who see your content and the total number of times it's viewed.
- **Follower Growth:** The rate at which you're gaining or losing followers.
- **Website Clicks:** The number of clicks on the link in your bio or post.
- **Story Views:** The number of views and interactions on your Stories.

Adapting Your Strategy

Use insights from your analytics to refine and adapt your content strategy. Identify patterns in high-performing content and replicate successful elements. Stay flexible and be willing to experiment with new types of content and features to keep your audience engaged.

By mastering content creation, you can build a strong, engaged community on Instagram and effectively market your products or services. In the next chapter, we will explore strategies for growing and engaging your audience to maximize your Instagram presence.

The Art of Visual Storytelling

Visual storytelling is a powerful tool for connecting with your audience on an emotional level and conveying your brand's message effectively. On Instagram, where visuals reign supreme, mastering this art can set your brand apart and foster a loyal following. This chapter delves into the principles and techniques of visual storytelling, helping you create compelling narratives that captivate and engage your audience.

Understanding Visual Storytelling

What is Visual Storytelling?

Visual storytelling involves using images, videos, and other visual elements to tell a story. It's about more than just posting beautiful photos; it's about creating a narrative that resonates with your audience and communicates your brand's values, mission, and personality.

Why Visual Storytelling Matters

1. **Emotional Connection:** Stories evoke emotions, and emotions drive engagement and loyalty. By telling a compelling story, you can create a deeper connection with your audience.

2. **Memorability:** People are more likely to remember stories than isolated facts or images. A strong narrative makes your brand more memorable.

3. **Engagement:** Stories encourage interaction. When followers feel part of your brand's journey, they're more likely to engage with your content.

4. Differentiation: In a crowded digital space, a unique story helps your brand stand out from the competition.

Elements of Effective Visual Storytelling

Authenticity

Authenticity is crucial in visual storytelling. Your audience can sense when something is genuine and when it's not. Share real moments, behind-the-scenes content, and user-generated content to build trust and authenticity.

Consistency

Consistency in style, tone, and messaging reinforces your brand identity and makes your content instantly recognizable. Use consistent color schemes, filters, and fonts to create a cohesive look.

Emotion

Appeal to emotions through your visuals and narratives. Happiness, nostalgia, inspiration, and excitement are powerful emotions that can drive engagement.

Simplicity

Keep your visuals clean and focused. Too much clutter can dilute your message. Use simple, strong images that convey your story effectively.

Relatability

Your audience should see themselves in your story. Understand their needs, challenges, and aspirations, and create content that reflects those.

Techniques for Visual Storytelling

Sequential Storytelling

Sequential storytelling involves breaking down a story into a series of posts or slides. This technique keeps your audience engaged and coming back for more. Use Instagram's carousel feature or stories to create a sequence.

Hero's Journey

The Hero's Journey is a classic storytelling structure where a hero embarks on an adventure, faces challenges, and returns transformed. Apply this structure to your brand's story or customer success stories to create compelling narratives.

Visual Metaphors

Use visual metaphors to convey complex ideas in a simple and relatable way. For example, a journey map can represent a customer's journey with your brand.

User-Generated Content

Encourage your customers to share their own stories featuring your products or services. User-generated content adds authenticity and provides diverse perspectives on your brand.

Crafting Your Visual Story

Identify Your Core Message

Start by defining the core message you want to convey. What do you want your audience to take away from your story? This could be your brand's mission, a product benefit, or an inspirational message.

Storyboarding

Plan your visual story through storyboarding. Sketch out each frame or post to visualize how the story will unfold. This helps in organizing your thoughts and ensuring a coherent narrative.

Scripting and Captions

Write a script for your story. Even in visual storytelling, the right words matter. Craft captions that complement your visuals and enhance the story. Use a consistent tone that aligns with your brand's voice.

Visual Composition

Pay attention to the composition of your visuals. Use the rule of thirds, leading lines, and symmetry to create aesthetically pleasing images. Ensure each visual element supports and enhances your story.

Editing and Enhancements

Edit your photos and videos to maintain a consistent style. Use filters, adjustments, and enhancements to achieve the desired look and feel. However, avoid over-editing, as it can detract from authenticity.

Integrating Brand Elements

Incorporate brand elements subtly within your visuals. This includes your logo, brand colors, and fonts. Ensure these elements do not overpower the visual but reinforce brand recognition.

Tools for Visual Storytelling

Photo and Video Editing Apps

Use apps like Adobe Lightroom, VSCO, and Snapseed for photo editing, and Adobe Premiere Rush or InShot for video editing. These tools offer a range of features to enhance your visuals.

Graphic Design Tools

Tools like Canva and Adobe Spark make it easy to create visually appealing graphics and infographics. Use them to add text overlays, create custom visuals, and design storyboards.

Storytelling Templates

Many graphic design tools offer templates for storyboards, carousel posts, and stories. Utilize these templates to streamline your visual storytelling process and maintain consistency.

Examples of Visual Storytelling

Brand Story

Share the history of your brand through a series of posts or a video. Highlight key milestones, challenges, and achievements. Use archival photos, behind-the-scenes footage, and interviews to add depth.

Product Launch

Announce a new product through a visual story. Show the product in development, highlight its features, and share customer testimonials. Use teasers to build anticipation and excitement.

Customer Journey

Tell the story of a customer's experience with your brand. Highlight their problem, how they discovered your brand, and how your product or service solved their issue. Use real customer stories and visuals.

Measuring the Impact of Visual Storytelling

Engagement Metrics

Track likes, comments, shares, and saves to gauge how well your story resonates with your audience. High engagement indicates that your story is effective.

Reach and Impressions

Monitor the reach and impressions of your story posts. A broad reach shows that your story is spreading, while high impressions indicate repeated views.

Follower Growth

An increase in followers after sharing a compelling story suggests that your content is attracting new audiences.

Feedback and Sentiment

Pay attention to comments and direct messages. Positive feedback and emotional responses indicate a successful visual story.

By mastering the art of visual storytelling, you can create content that not only captures attention but also builds a lasting connection with your audience. In the next chapter, we will explore advanced strategies for growing and engaging your audience to maximize your Instagram presence.

Creating High-Quality Posts and Stories

Creating high-quality posts and stories is essential for maintaining an engaging and professional Instagram presence. High-quality content not only attracts new followers but also keeps your current audience interested and engaged. In this chapter, we'll explore the techniques and best practices for creating visually appealing and impactful posts and stories.

High-Quality Posts

Photography Tips

1. Lighting:
- **Natural Light:** The best source for photography. Aim to shoot during the golden hours (early morning or late afternoon) for soft, flattering light.
- **Artificial Light:** Use softboxes or ring lights to replicate natural light. Avoid harsh overhead lighting that can create unflattering shadows.

2. Composition:
- **Rule of Thirds:** Divide your image into nine equal parts using two horizontal and two vertical lines. Place key elements along these lines or at their intersections.
- **Leading Lines:** Use natural lines in your photos to guide the viewer's eye towards the main subject.

- **Symmetry and Balance:** Symmetrical compositions can be pleasing to the eye. Balance your composition by ensuring that elements are evenly distributed within the frame.

3. Background:

- Keep backgrounds clean and uncluttered to ensure your subject stands out.
- Use backgrounds that complement but do not overpower your subject.

4. Consistency:

- Maintain a consistent visual style to create a cohesive look across your posts. This could involve using the same filters, color schemes, or editing techniques.

Editing Techniques

1. Brightness and Contrast:

- Adjust brightness and contrast to make your images pop. Be careful not to overexpose or underexpose your photos.

2. Color Correction:

- Adjust the color balance to achieve natural-looking tones. Use saturation and vibrance adjustments to enhance colors.

3. Sharpness and Clarity:

- Increase sharpness to bring out details. Use clarity adjustments sparingly to avoid making the image look too harsh.

4. Filters and Presets:

- Use filters and presets to create a consistent look. Avoid overly dramatic filters that can detract from the natural beauty of your images.

Caption Writing

1. Voice and Tone:

- Write captions that reflect your brand's voice. Whether it's formal, casual, witty, or inspirational, consistency is key.

2. Engagement:

- Encourage engagement by asking questions, prompting followers to share their thoughts, or directing them to your bio link.

3. Length:

- Instagram allows up to 2,200 characters, but focuses on making your captions concise and impactful. The first sentence should grab attention, as it's what appears in the feed preview.

4. Calls to Action (CTA):

- Include clear CTAs, such as asking followers to comment, share, or visit your website.

Hashtags

1. Relevance:

- Use hashtags that are relevant to your content and industry to attract the right audience.

2. Mix of Popular and Niche:

- Combine popular hashtags with niche ones to increase visibility while targeting a specific audience.

3. Branded Hashtags:

- Create a unique hashtag for your brand to encourage user-generated content and community building.

4. Number of Hashtags:

- Instagram allows up to 30 hashtags per post, but the optimal number is typically between 5 and 11 for balanced reach and engagement.

High-Quality Stories

Story Ideas

1. Behind-the-Scenes:

- Share behind-the-scenes content to give your audience a glimpse into your brand's daily operations and culture.

2. Tutorials and How-Tos:

- Create step-by-step guides or tutorials to provide value and showcase your expertise.

3. User-Generated Content:

- Share content created by your followers to build community and show appreciation.

4. Polls and Questions:

- Use interactive elements like polls and question stickers to engage your audience and gather feedback.

Design Tips

1. Templates:

- Use story templates to maintain a consistent and professional look. Tools like Canva and Adobe Spark offer customizable templates for Instagram Stories.

2. Text and Fonts:

- Use clear and readable fonts. Highlight important information by varying font sizes and styles.

3. Colors:

- Use your brand's color palette to create a cohesive look. Ensure that text stands out against the background.

4. Stickers and GIFs:

- Use stickers, GIFs, and emojis to add personality and engagement. Avoid overloading your story with too many elements.

Storytelling Techniques

1. Sequential Storytelling:

- Break down your story into a series of posts to keep your audience engaged. Use each frame to build on the previous one, creating a narrative flow.

2. Hooks and Teasers:

- Start with a hook to grab attention. Use teasers to build anticipation for upcoming content.

3. Calls to Action (CTA):

- Include CTAs to encourage interaction. This could be as simple as swiping up for a link (if you have the feature) or directing followers to DM you for more information.

Highlights

1. Organize by Category:
   - Group your stories into highlights based on categories such as products, tutorials, customer reviews, and events.

2. Custom Covers:
   - Use custom highlight covers that align with your brand's visual style. This makes your profile look organized and professional.

3. Regular Updates:
   - Update your highlights regularly to keep them relevant and up-to-date with your latest and best content.

Tools for Creating High-Quality Content

Photo and Video Editing Apps

1. Adobe Lightroom:

 - Offers advanced editing features and presets to enhance your photos.

2. VSCO:

 - Provides a wide range of filters and editing tools to create a cohesive look.

3. Snapseed:

 - A user-friendly app with powerful editing capabilities.

Graphic Design Tools

1. Canva:

 - Easy-to-use design tool with templates for posts and stories.

2. Adobe Spark:

 - Offers templates and customization options for creating engaging visuals.

3. Over:

 - Allows you to add text, graphics, and effects to your photos and videos.

Story Templates

1. Unfold:

- Offers minimalist templates for creating clean and stylish stories.

2. StoryArt:

- Provides a variety of templates and themes to make your stories stand out.

3. Mojo:

- Create animated stories with customizable templates.

By following these guidelines and utilizing the right tools, you can create high-quality posts and stories that captivate your audience, enhance your brand's image, and drive engagement on Instagram. In the next chapter, we will explore advanced strategies for growing and engaging your audience to maximize your Instagram presence.

Leveraging Instagram Reels and IGTV

Instagram Reels and IGTV are powerful tools for reaching and engaging your audience with dynamic video content. Understanding how to effectively use these features can help you amplify your brand's presence on Instagram and connect with your followers in new and impactful ways. This chapter will explore strategies for creating compelling Reels and IGTV videos, as well as best practices for leveraging these formats to grow your audience.

Instagram Reels

What Are Instagram Reels?

Instagram Reels are short, engaging videos that can be up to 60 seconds long. They offer a fun and creative way to share content, with features such as music, text overlays, and various effects. Reels appear in a dedicated section on your profile and can be discovered through the Explore page, providing significant opportunities for increased visibility.

Creating Engaging Reels

1. Identify Your Audience:

- Understand who your target audience is and what type of content they find entertaining and valuable. Tailor your Reels to their interests and preferences.

2. Plan Your Content:

- Develop a content plan that outlines the themes and topics you'll cover in your Reels. Consider trends, challenges, and relevant hashtags to increase discoverability.

3. Script and Storyboard:

- Outline the key points of your Reel and create a storyboard to visualize the sequence. This helps ensure a smooth flow and coherent message.

4. Use Music and Sound:

- Choose trending music or sound effects to enhance your Reels. Music can set the tone and make your videos more engaging.

5. Add Text and Effects:

- Use text overlays to highlight important information and add context. Explore Instagram's effects and filters to make your Reels visually appealing.

6. Incorporate Trends:

- Participate in popular trends and challenges to increase your Reels' chances of being featured on the Explore page. Stay updated with the latest trends in your niche.

Types of Content for Reels

1. How-To Tutorials:

- Create quick, step-by-step tutorials that provide value to your audience. For example, show how to use a product or share tips related to your industry.

2. Behind-the-Scenes:

- Give followers a peek behind the curtain by showcasing your workplace, team, or production process. This builds authenticity and trust.

3. Product Showcases:

- Highlight your products in action. Demonstrate their features and benefits in a creative and engaging way.

4. User-Generated Content:

- Feature content created by your followers to build community and credibility. Reposting customer reviews or testimonials can be very effective.

5. Entertainment:

- Share fun and entertaining content that aligns with your brand's personality. This can include challenges, funny skits, or creative animations.

Best Practices for Reels

1. Keep It Short and Sweet:

- Attention spans are short on social media. Aim to deliver your message concisely within the 60-second limit.

2. Hook Your Audience Early:

- Capture attention within the first few seconds. Use an intriguing opening to encourage viewers to watch the entire Reel.

3. Consistency:

- Post Reels regularly to keep your audience engaged. Consistency helps maintain visibility and follower interest.

4. Engage with Comments:

- Respond to comments on your Reels to build community and encourage further engagement. Engaging with your audience fosters loyalty and interaction.

IGTV

What is IGTV?

IGTV (Instagram TV) is a platform for sharing long-form videos on Instagram. Videos can be up to 60 minutes long for verified accounts, making IGTV ideal for more in-depth content such as tutorials, interviews, and webinars. IGTV videos can be accessed through a dedicated tab on your profile and the IGTV app.

Creating High-Quality IGTV Videos

1. Plan Your Content:

- Develop a content calendar for IGTV, planning topics that provide value to your audience. Consider what type of long-form content your followers would find useful and engaging.

2. Script and Outline:

- Write a detailed script or outline to ensure your video is structured and stays on topic. Plan your introduction, main points, and conclusion.

3. Professional Production:

- Invest in good equipment, such as a high-quality camera and microphone, to ensure your videos look and sound professional. Pay attention to lighting and background to enhance video quality.

4. Engaging Thumbnails:

- Create eye-catching thumbnails that accurately represent your video's content. Thumbnails are the first thing viewers see, so make them compelling.

Types of Content for IGTV

1. In-Depth Tutorials:

- Create detailed tutorials that walk viewers through complex processes or skills. This format allows you to provide comprehensive value.

2. Interviews and Q&A Sessions:

- Host interviews with industry experts or conduct Q&A sessions with your audience. This type of content can position your brand as a thought leader.

3. Product Demonstrations:

- Showcase your products in detail, explaining features and benefits. This is especially useful for new product launches.

4. Webinars and Workshops:

- Share educational content through webinars or workshops. These can be pre-recorded or live, offering an interactive experience for your audience.

Best Practices for IGTV

1. Promote Your Videos:
- Use Instagram Stories, posts, and other social media platforms to promote your IGTV videos. Encourage your followers to watch and share.

2. Engage with Your Audience:
- Respond to comments and engage with viewers. Answer questions and acknowledge feedback to build a strong community.

3. Cross-Promote Content:
- Link to your IGTV videos in your Instagram bio and other social media profiles. Cross-promotion helps drive traffic to your IGTV channel.

4. Analyze Performance:

- Use Instagram's analytics to track the performance of your IGTV videos. Monitor metrics such as views, engagement, and audience retention to understand what works and what doesn't.

Examples of Successful Reels and IGTV Content

1. Reels:

- **Sephora:** Shares quick makeup tutorials and product showcases, leveraging popular music and trends to engage followers.
- **Nike:** Uses motivational content and highlights athletes' stories, combining stunning visuals and powerful messages.

2. IGTV:

- **National Geographic:** Produces in-depth documentaries and behind-the-scenes content, offering educational and visually rich experiences.
- **Glossier:** Features detailed product demonstrations, customer testimonials, and Q&A sessions with experts.

By leveraging Instagram Reels and IGTV, you can create dynamic, engaging content that reaches a broader audience and strengthens your brand's presence on Instagram. In the next chapter, we will explore advanced strategies for growing and engaging your audience to maximize your Instagram presence.

Developing a Content Calendar

A well-planned content calendar is essential for maintaining a consistent and engaging Instagram presence. It helps you organize your content, ensure variety, and align your posts with your marketing goals. In this chapter, we will explore how to develop an effective content calendar that keeps your audience engaged and supports your overall strategy.

Why a Content Calendar Matters

1. Consistency:

- Regular posting keeps your audience engaged and helps you stay top of mind. A content calendar ensures you maintain a consistent posting schedule.

2. Strategic Planning:

- A calendar allows you to plan content around key dates, events, and marketing campaigns, ensuring your posts align with your business goals.

3. Content Variety:

- By planning ahead, you can ensure a good mix of content types (photos, videos, stories, Reels, IGTV) and themes (educational, promotional, user-generated content).

4. Efficiency:

- Having a content calendar streamlines your workflow, saving time and reducing the stress of last-minute content creation.

Steps to Develop a Content Calendar

1. Set Your Goals

Identify the primary objectives you want to achieve with your Instagram content. Goals could include increasing brand awareness, driving website traffic, generating leads, or boosting engagement.

2. Understand Your Audience

Analyze your audience demographics, preferences, and behaviors. Use Instagram Insights and other analytics tools to gather data on what types of content resonate most with your followers.

3. Identify Key Dates and Events

Include important dates such as product launches, holidays, industry events, and company milestones. Plan content around these dates to leverage their significance.

4. Determine Content Themes and Types

Decide on the main themes and content types you want to include in your calendar. Common content types include:

- **Photos and Graphics:** High-quality images that showcase your products, services, or brand personality.
- **Videos:** Short clips, tutorials, behind-the-scenes footage, and testimonials.
- **Stories:** Temporary posts that provide updates, announcements, and interactive content.
- **Reels:** Short, engaging videos that leverage trends and music.
- **IGTV:** Long-form videos for in-depth tutorials, interviews, and webinars.
- **User-Generated Content:** Content created by your followers, showcasing their experiences with your brand.

5. Create a Posting Schedule

Determine how often you want to post on Instagram. Consistency is key, but quality should never be sacrificed for quantity. A typical posting frequency might be:

- **Feed Posts:** 3-5 times per week.
- **Stories:** Daily or several times a week.
- **Reels:** 1-3 times per week.
- **IGTV:** 1-2 times per month.

6. Plan Content in Advance

Using a calendar tool, plot out your content ideas for each day, week, or month. Tools like Google Calendar, Trello, Asana, or dedicated social media management tools like Hootsuite, Later, and Buffer can help you organize your content schedule.

7. Develop Content

Start creating the content you've planned. Write captions, design graphics, shoot photos, and produce videos. Ensure all content aligns with your brand's voice and style.

8. Review and Adjust

Regularly review the performance of your content using Instagram Insights and other analytics tools. Adjust your content calendar based on what works best, and stay flexible to accommodate new trends and opportunities.

Example of a Monthly Content Calendar

Week 1

- **Monday:** Inspirational Quote (Photo)
- **Tuesday:** Product Highlight (Reel)
- **Wednesday:** Behind-the-Scenes (Story)
- **Thursday:** User-Generated Content (Photo)
- **Friday:** Fun Fact or Industry News (Graphic)
- **Saturday:** Weekend Giveaway Announcement (Photo)
- **Sunday:** Q&A Session (Story)

Week 2

- **Monday:** Customer Testimonial (Video)
- **Tuesday:** Tutorial (IGTV)

- **Wednesday:** Midweek Motivation (Reel)
- **Thursday:** Poll or Quiz (Story)
- **Friday:** Flash Sale Announcement (Photo)
- **Saturday:** Event Highlight (Story)
- **Sunday:** Weekly Recap (Story)

Week 3

- ***Monday:** Blog Post Promotion (Photo)
- **Tuesday:** New Product Teaser (Reel)
- **Wednesday:** Team Spotlight (Story)
- **Thursday:** Throwback Thursday (Photo)
- **Friday:** Product Demo (Video)
- **Saturday:** Contest Launch (Photo)
- **Sunday:** Influencer Collaboration (Story)

Week 4

- **Monday:** Motivational Monday (Quote Graphic)
- **Tuesday:** How-To Guide (Reel)
- **Wednesday:** FAQ (Story)
- **Thursday:** Customer Spotlight (Photo)
- **Friday:** Feature Friday (Highlight a popular product) (Photo)

- **Saturday:** Behind-the-Scenes (Video)

- **Sunday:** Sunday Fun (Interactive Story - Polls/Questions)

Tools for Managing Your Content Calendar

1. Google Calendar

Use Google Calendar to schedule your posts and set reminders. It's a straightforward tool for planning and keeping track of your content.

2. Trello

Trello offers a visual way to organize your content ideas and schedule. Create boards, lists, and cards for each content type and plan.

3. Asana

Asana helps with task management and allows you to plan, assign, and track content creation tasks within your team.

4. Hootsuite

Hootsuite is a comprehensive social media management tool that lets you schedule and publish content across multiple platforms. It also provides analytics to track performance.

5. Later

Later specializes in Instagram scheduling, offering a visual content calendar, media library, and analytics. It's designed to help you plan and publish Instagram posts effectively.

6. Buffer

Buffer allows you to schedule posts, analyze performance, and manage all your social media accounts in one place. It's user-friendly and efficient for content planning.

Tips for Maintaining Your Content Calendar

1. Batch Content Creation:

- Create content in batches to save time and ensure you have a backlog of posts ready to go.

2. Stay Flexible:

- Be prepared to adjust your calendar as needed. Trends and opportunities can arise suddenly, requiring you to pivot your plans.

3. Monitor and Adjust:

- Regularly review your content's performance and adjust your strategy based on what resonates most with your audience.

4. Collaborate with Your Team:

- Involve your team in content planning and creation. Diverse perspectives can enhance your content and ensure it aligns with your brand's goals.

5. Engage with Your Audience:

- Use your content calendar to plan engagement strategies, such as responding to comments, running contests, and featuring user-generated content.

By developing and maintaining a robust content calendar, you can ensure a steady flow of high-quality, engaging content that supports your brand's goals and resonates with your audience. In the next chapter, we will explore advanced strategies for analyzing and optimizing your Instagram performance.

Using Hashtags Effectively

Hashtags are a powerful tool for expanding your reach and engaging with a broader audience on Instagram. They help categorize your content, making it discoverable to users interested in specific topics. This chapter will guide you through the strategies for using hashtags effectively to maximize your Instagram marketing efforts.

The Importance of Hashtags

1. Increased Visibility:
   - Hashtags make your content discoverable to a wider audience beyond your followers. When users

search for or follow a hashtag, your posts can appear in their feed.

2. Enhanced Engagement:

- Posts with relevant hashtags tend to receive more likes, comments, and shares because they reach users who are genuinely interested in the content.

3. Brand Awareness:

- Creating and promoting a branded hashtag can help build community and encourage user-generated content, increasing your brand's visibility and credibility.

4. Targeted Reach:

- Using specific hashtags related to your niche or industry helps you reach a targeted audience that is more likely to be interested in your products or services.

Types of Hashtags

1. Branded Hashtags

Branded hashtags are unique to your business and are used to promote your brand and campaigns. They can be your company name, tagline, or a specific campaign.

- **Example:** #JustDoIt (Nike), #ShareACoke (Coca-Cola)

2. Industry Hashtags

These hashtags are related to your industry or niche. They help connect with others in your field and attract users interested in industry-specific content.

- **Example:** #DigitalMarketing, #FitnessTips

3. Community Hashtags

Community hashtags are used to join larger conversations and engage with specific communities on Instagram. These hashtags help you connect with like-minded users.

- Example: #InstaTravel, #Foodie

4. Campaign Hashtags

Campaign hashtags are specific to marketing campaigns or events. They are typically used for a limited time to promote a particular initiative.

- Example: #BlackFridayDeals, #SummerSale

5. Trending Hashtags

Trending hashtags are currently popular and widely used. Leveraging these can increase your visibility, but ensure they are relevant to your content.

- Example: #ThrowbackThursday, #OOTD (Outfit of the Day)

6. Location Hashtags

Location hashtags include geographic locations to attract local users or people interested in a particular area.

- **Example:** #NYC, #LondonEats

7. Event Hashtags

Event hashtags are used to promote or engage with specific events, conferences, or holidays.

- **Example:** #CES2024, #WorldCup2024

Strategies for Effective Hashtag Use

1. Research Relevant Hashtags

1. Analyze Competitors:
   - Look at the hashtags used by your competitors and industry leaders. This can give you insights into popular and effective hashtags in your niche.

2. Use Instagram's Search Function:

- Use Instagram's search bar to find hashtags related to your content. Look at the number of posts associated with each hashtag to gauge its popularity.

3. Explore Hashtag Tools:

- Use tools like Hashtagify, RiteTag, and All Hashtag to find relevant hashtags and analyze their performance.

2. Mix Popular and Niche Hashtags

1. Popular Hashtags:

- These have a large number of posts and can increase your visibility. However, they are highly competitive.

2. Niche Hashtags:

- These are more specific and have fewer posts. They help you reach a more targeted audience with less competition.

3. Use a Variety of Hashtags

1. Combine Different Types:

- Use a mix of branded, industry, community, and location hashtags to broaden your reach.

2. Optimal Number:

- Instagram allows up to 30 hashtags per post, but studies suggest using 5-11 relevant hashtags to maximize engagement without overwhelming your audience.

4. Create and Promote a Branded Hashtag

1. Unique and Memorable:

- Ensure your branded hashtag is unique, easy to remember, and relevant to your brand.

2. Encourage Usage:

- Promote your branded hashtag in your bio, posts, stories, and marketing materials. Encourage your followers to use it when sharing content related to your brand.

5. Monitor and Adjust

1. Track Performance:

- Use Instagram Insights and other analytics tools to monitor the performance of your hashtags. Track metrics such as reach, engagement, and follower growth.

2. Adjust Accordingly:

- Based on your analysis, adjust your hashtag strategy to focus on those that perform best and align with your marketing goals.

6. Avoid Banned or Overused Hashtags

1. Banned Hashtags:

- Instagram occasionally bans hashtags that are associated with inappropriate content or behavior. Using banned hashtags can reduce your post's visibility.

2. Overused Hashtags:

- Avoid overly generic hashtags like #love or #instagood, as they are saturated and unlikely to help your content stand out.

Best Practices for Hashtag Use

1. Placement of Hashtags

1. In the Caption:

- Place hashtags directly in your caption. This keeps everything in one place and can make your post more discoverable.

2. In the Comments:

- Alternatively, you can place hashtags in the first comment to keep your caption clean. This doesn't affect the discoverability of your post.

2. Keep Your Hashtags Relevant

1. Context Matters:

- Ensure your hashtags are relevant to the content of your post. Irrelevant hashtags can confuse users and lead to lower engagement.

2. Stay Authentic:

- Use hashtags that genuinely relate to your brand and content. Authenticity builds trust and credibility with your audience.

3. Engage with Hashtag Communities

1. Like and Comment:

- Engage with posts under the hashtags you use. Like and comment on relevant posts to build relationships and increase your visibility within those communities.

2. Follow Hashtags:

- Follow hashtags relevant to your industry to stay updated with trends and engage with content from other users.

4. Refresh Your Hashtag Strategy Regularly

1. Stay Updated:

- Hashtag trends can change. Regularly update your hashtag strategy to include new and trending hashtags relevant to your audience.

2. Test and Learn:

- Experiment with different combinations of hashtags and analyze the results. Learning from these tests can help you refine your strategy.

Example of Effective Hashtag Use

Post: Promoting a New Fitness Product

- **Caption:** "Achieve your fitness goals with our latest #WorkoutGear! Available now. #FitnessGoals #HealthyLifestyle #GymLife"
- **Hashtags in Caption:** #WorkoutGear, #FitnessGoals, #HealthyLifestyle, #GymLife
- **Hashtags in First Comment:** #FitnessAddict, #FitFam, #Exercise, #GetFit, #FitnessMotivation, #Health, #Wellness, #ActiveLife, #StrengthTraining, #FitnessCommunity

Post: Behind-the-Scenes of a Fashion Photoshoot

- **Caption:** "Behind the scenes of our latest collection photoshoot! ☐ #FashionPhotoshoot #BTS #FashionInspo"
- **Hashtags in Caption:** #FashionPhotoshoot, #BTS, #FashionInspo
- **Hashtags in First Comment:** #FashionPhotography, #BehindTheScenes, #Style, #FashionBlogger, #OOTD, #FashionGram, #ModelLife, #FashionDesigner, #CreativeDirector, #PhotoShoot

By using hashtags effectively, you can significantly enhance your Instagram presence, reach a wider audience, and engage more deeply with your followers. In the next chapter, we will delve into advanced strategies for growing and engaging your audience to maximize your Instagram marketing efforts.

Chapter 3: Building and Engaging Your Audience

Creating a strong and engaged Instagram audience is essential for successful marketing. A dedicated audience not only increases your reach but also helps in building brand loyalty and driving conversions. This chapter will cover strategies for growing your audience and keeping them actively engaged with your content.

Understanding Your Audience

1. Define Your Target Audience

1. Demographics:

 - Identify the age, gender, location, and other demographic factors of your target audience. This helps tailor your content to their preferences and interests.

2. Interests and Behaviors:

- Understand what your audience cares about, including their hobbies, values, and purchasing behaviors. Use this information to create content that resonates with them.

3. Pain Points and Needs:

- Identify the challenges and needs of your audience. Providing solutions to their problems can make your content more valuable and engaging.

2. Use Instagram Insights

1. Follower Demographics:

- Use Instagram Insights to analyze your current followers' demographics. This data provides valuable information on who is engaging with your content.

2. Content Performance:

- Track which types of content perform best in terms of reach, likes, comments, and shares. Use this data to refine your content strategy.

Strategies for Growing Your Audience

1. Optimize Your Profile

1. Profile Picture:

- Use a high-quality image that represents your brand. For businesses, a logo or recognizable brand image works best.

2. Bio:

- Write a compelling bio that clearly explains who you are and what you offer. Include relevant keywords and a call to action, such as a link to your website.

3. Contact Information:

- Make it easy for people to contact you by including an email address, phone number, and business address (if applicable).

2. Post High-Quality Content

1. Consistency:

- Post regularly to keep your audience engaged. Create a content calendar to plan and schedule your posts in advance.

2. Visual Appeal:

- Use high-quality images and videos. Invest in good photography and editing tools to enhance your content.

3. Variety:

- Mix up your content types, including photos, videos, stories, Reels, and IGTV. This keeps your feed interesting and engaging.

3. Use Hashtags Strategically

1. Relevant Hashtags:

- Use a mix of popular, niche, and branded hashtags to increase your content's discoverability. Refer to the previous chapter for detailed hashtag strategies.

2. Trending Hashtags:

- Stay updated with trending hashtags related to your industry. Participating in popular trends can boost your visibility.

4. Engage with Your Followers

1. Respond to Comments:

- Engage with your audience by responding to comments on your posts. This shows that you value their input and encourages more interaction.

2. Like and Comment:

- Actively engage with your followers' content by liking and commenting on their posts. This helps build a community and encourages reciprocation.

3. Direct Messages:

- Use direct messages to have one-on-one conversations with your followers. Personal interactions can build stronger connections.

5. Collaborate with Influencers

1. Identify Relevant Influencers:

- Find influencers in your industry with a similar target audience. Ensure their values and content style align with your brand.

2. Collaborative Content:

- Work with influencers to create content, such as sponsored posts, takeovers, or joint giveaways. Influencer collaborations can expose your brand to a wider audience.

6. Run Contests and Giveaways

1. Clear Rules:

- Clearly outline the rules and entry requirements for your contest or giveaway. Make it easy for users to participate.

2. Engaging Prizes:

- Offer prizes that are valuable and relevant to your audience. This increases participation and excitement.

3. Promotion:

- Promote your contest or giveaway through your posts, stories, and other social media channels. Encourage participants to share with their followers.

7. Utilize Instagram Stories

1. Daily Updates:
- Use Stories to provide daily updates, behind-the-scenes content, and time-sensitive information. Stories keep your audience engaged between regular posts.

2. Interactive Features:
- Use interactive features like polls, quizzes, and questions to engage with your audience. These features encourage participation and feedback.

3. Highlight Reels:
- Save important Stories in Highlight Reels on your profile. Highlights allow new followers to catch up on key content and get to know your brand.

Strategies for Engaging Your Audience

1. Create Valuable Content

1. Educational Content:

 - Share tips, tutorials, and how-to guides that provide value to your audience. Educational content establishes your brand as an authority in your industry.

2. Entertaining Content:

 - Post fun and entertaining content that aligns with your brand's voice. This could include memes, humorous videos, or entertaining stories.

3. Inspirational Content:

 - Share motivational quotes, success stories, and inspirational messages. Positive content can boost engagement and create a sense of community.

2. Encourage User-Generated Content

1. Create a Branded Hashtag:

 - Encourage your followers to use a branded hashtag when they post content related to your brand. Reposting user-generated content builds community and trust.

2. Feature Customers:

- Showcase your customers using your products or services. Highlighting customer stories and testimonials can increase engagement and loyalty.

3. Host Live Sessions

1. Live Q&A:

- Host live Q&A sessions to answer your followers' questions in real-time. This interactive format fosters a direct connection with your audience.

2. Product Launches:

- Use live sessions to announce and demonstrate new products. Live reveals create excitement and immediate feedback.

3. Collaborations:

- Co-host live sessions with influencers or industry experts. Collaborative lives can draw in new followers and provide diverse content.

4. Use Polls and Questions

1. Polls:

- Use polls in your Stories to gather opinions and feedback from your audience. Polls are an easy way to increase interaction.

2. Questions:

- Use the question sticker in Stories to invite your followers to ask you anything. Responding to questions shows that you value their input and are approachable.

5. Share Behind-the-Scenes Content

1. Company Culture:

- Share behind-the-scenes glimpses of your company culture, team activities, and workplace environment. This humanizes your brand and builds trust.

2. Product Development:

- Show the process of how your products are made, from concept to creation. Transparency can increase customer appreciation and loyalty.

6. Post at Optimal Times

1. Analyze Data:

- Use Instagram Insights to determine when your audience is most active. Posting at these times can increase visibility and engagement.

2. Experiment:

- Test different posting times to see when your audience is most responsive. Adjust your schedule based on your findings.

7. Encourage Engagement

1. Call to Action:

- Include clear calls to action in your captions, such as asking questions, prompting followers to tag friends, or encouraging them to share their thoughts.

2. Engagement Contests:

  - Run contests that require engagement, such as liking, commenting, or sharing your post. This boosts interaction and extends your reach.

Measuring Engagement Success

1. Track Key Metrics

1. Likes and Comments:

  - Monitor the number of likes and comments on your posts. High engagement indicates that your content resonates with your audience.

2. Shares and Saves:

  - Track how often your posts are shared or saved. These actions indicate that your content is valuable and worth keeping.

3. Story Views:

- Analyze the number of views your Stories receive. High view counts suggest that your Stories are engaging and relevant.

4. Follower Growth:

- Measure your follower growth over time. Steady growth indicates a successful engagement strategy.

2. Use Analytics Tools

1. Instagram Insights:

- Use Instagram's built-in analytics to track engagement metrics and audience demographics. Insights provide valuable data to refine your strategy.

2. Third-Party Tools:

- Use tools like Hootsuite, Sprout Social, or Buffer to gain deeper insights into your engagement metrics and overall performance.

3. Adjust Your Strategy

1. Analyze Performance:

- Regularly review your engagement metrics to identify trends and patterns. Understand what types of content perform best and why.

2. Experiment and Iterate:

- Continuously experiment with different content types, posting times, and engagement strategies. Use your findings to refine and improve your approach.

By implementing these strategies, you can effectively build and engage your Instagram audience, fostering a loyal community that supports your brand's growth. In the next chapter, we will explore advanced tactics for leveraging Instagram analytics to optimize your marketing efforts.

Strategies for Growing Your Follower Base

Increasing your follower base on Instagram requires a combination of strategic planning, engaging content, and active community involvement. This chapter provides actionable strategies to help you grow your Instagram followers organically and build a loyal, engaged audience.

Optimize Your Profile

1. Use a Recognizable Profile Picture

- **Brand Logo:** Use a clear and high-resolution version of your brand's logo. This helps in building brand recognition.
- **Personal Brand:** If you are a personal brand or influencer, use a high-quality photo that clearly shows your face.

2. Craft a Compelling Bio

- **Clear and Concise:** Explain who you are and what you offer in a few short sentences. Use keywords related to your niche.
- **Include a Call to Action:** Encourage visitors to take action, such as visiting your website, signing

up for your newsletter, or checking out your latest post.

- Add Contact Information: Make it easy for people to contact you by including your email, phone number, or business address.

3. Utilize Profile Links

- Link to Your Website: Use the link in your bio to drive traffic to your website, blog, or a specific landing page.

- Linktree or Similar Tools: Use tools like Linktree to add multiple links in your bio, directing followers to various resources.

Create High-Quality Content

1. Focus on Visual Appeal

- High-Resolution Images and Videos: Always use high-quality visuals. Invest in good photography and videography tools.

- **Consistent Aesthetic:** Maintain a consistent style, color scheme, and theme across your posts to create a cohesive look.

2. Provide Value

- **Educational Content:** Share tips, tutorials, and informative posts that add value to your followers' lives.
- **Entertaining Content:** Post entertaining videos, memes, or humorous content that aligns with your brand's voice.
- **Inspirational Content:** Share motivational quotes, success stories, and uplifting messages to engage and inspire your audience.

3. Post Regularly

- **Consistent Posting Schedule:** Develop a posting schedule and stick to it. Consistency keeps your audience engaged and coming back for more.
- **Optimal Posting Times:** Use Instagram Insights to determine when your audience is most active and post during those times.

Engage with Your Audience

1. Respond to Comments

- **Active Engagement:** Respond to comments on your posts to show appreciation and encourage more interaction.
- **Thoughtful Replies:** Provide meaningful and thoughtful replies to foster deeper connections with your followers.

2. Engage with Other Users

- **Like and Comment:** Actively like and comment on posts from other users in your niche. This increases your visibility and builds relationships.
- **Follow Relevant Accounts:** Follow accounts that are relevant to your niche. Engaging with their content can attract their followers to your profile.

3. Use Instagram Stories and Live Sessions

- Behind-the-Scenes Content: Share behind-the-scenes content and daily updates through Stories to keep your audience engaged.

- Interactive Features: Use polls, questions, and quizzes in Stories to interact with your followers.

- Live Sessions: Host live Q&A sessions, product launches, or collaborations to engage with your audience in real-time.

Leverage Hashtags

1. Use Relevant Hashtags

- Industry-Specific Hashtags: Use hashtags that are specific to your industry or niche to reach a targeted audience.

- Branded Hashtags: Create and promote a unique hashtag for your brand to build community and encourage user-generated content.

2. Mix Popular and Niche Hashtags

- **Popular Hashtags:** Include a few popular hashtags to increase your reach, but avoid overly saturated ones.

- **Niche Hashtags:** Use niche hashtags to connect with a more targeted and engaged audience.

3. Research and Experiment

- **Hashtag Research:** Use tools like Hashtagify, RiteTag, and All Hashtag to find relevant hashtags and analyze their performance.

- **Test Different Combinations:** Experiment with different hashtag combinations to see which ones generate the most engagement.

Collaborate with Influencers

1. Identify Relevant Influencers

- **Research Influencers:** Find influencers in your niche who have a similar target audience and align with your brand values.

- **Check Engagement:** Choose influencers with high engagement rates, not just a large number of followers.

2. Develop Collaborative Content

- **Sponsored Posts:** Partner with influencers to create sponsored posts that showcase your products or services.
- **Takeovers and Joint Giveaways:** Host Instagram takeovers or joint giveaways to tap into the influencer's audience.

3. Measure Success

- **Track Performance:** Monitor the performance of influencer collaborations through metrics such as engagement, follower growth, and conversions.
- **Adjust Strategy:** Use the insights gained to refine your influencer marketing strategy for future collaborations.

Run Contests and Giveaways

1. Plan Your Contest

- **Clear Goals:** Define the objectives of your contest, whether it's to increase followers, boost engagement, or promote a product.
- **Simple Entry Requirements:** Make it easy for users to participate by setting simple entry requirements, such as liking a post, tagging friends, or following your account.

2. Promote Your Contest

- **Create Engaging Graphics:** Design eye-catching graphics to promote your contest across your feed, Stories, and other social media platforms.
- **Collaborate with Influencers:** Partner with influencers to promote your contest and reach a wider audience.

3. Announce Winners and Showcase Participation

- Announce Publicly: Announce the winners publicly to maintain transparency and encourage more participation in future contests.

- Share User-Generated Content: Highlight user-generated content from participants to build community and showcase engagement.

Utilize Instagram Ads

1. Define Your Ad Objectives

- Set Clear Goals: Determine the primary goal of your Instagram ads, such as increasing brand awareness, driving website traffic, or generating leads.

- Target Audience: Define your target audience based on demographics, interests, and behaviors.

2. Create Compelling Ads

- High-Quality Visuals: Use high-quality images or videos that grab attention and align with your brand's aesthetic.

- **Strong Call to Action:** Include a clear and compelling call to action that encourages users to take the desired action.

3. Monitor and Optimize

- **Track Performance:** Use Instagram Insights and Facebook Ads Manager to monitor the performance of your ads.
- **Optimize Campaigns:** Adjust your ad campaigns based on performance data to improve results and maximize your return on investment.

Cross-Promote on Other Platforms

1. Leverage Your Existing Audience

- **Promote on Other Social Media:** Share your Instagram content on other social media platforms like Facebook, Twitter, and LinkedIn to drive traffic to your Instagram profile.
- **Email Marketing:** Include your Instagram handle in your email signature and newsletters to

encourage your email subscribers to follow you on Instagram.

2. Collaborate with Brands

- **Co-Promotions:** Partner with other brands for co-promotions or cross-marketing campaigns. This helps you reach a broader audience and gain new followers.

3. Utilize Influencer Networks

- **Influencer Partnerships:** Collaborate with influencers who have a presence on multiple platforms to promote your Instagram account across their social media channels.

By implementing these strategies, you can effectively grow your Instagram follower base, creating a larger, more engaged audience for your brand. In the next chapter, we will explore advanced tactics for analyzing and optimizing your Instagram performance to ensure continuous growth and engagement.

Engaging with Your Audience

Engagement is the key to building a loyal and active community on Instagram. Interacting with your audience not only fosters relationships but also enhances your brand's visibility and credibility. This chapter delves into effective strategies for engaging with your Instagram followers to create a vibrant and engaged community.

Responding to Comments

1. Be Timely

- **Quick Responses:** Aim to respond to comments as soon as possible. Timely responses show that you value your audience's input and are actively engaged with your community.
- **Notifications:** Turn on notifications for your posts to stay updated on new comments and engage promptly.

2. Be Personal and Genuine

- **Personal Touch:** Address commenters by their names and personalize your responses to make them feel valued.
- **Show Authenticity:** Be genuine in your replies. Avoid generic or automated responses to create meaningful interactions.

3. Encourage Further Interaction

- **Ask Questions:** Encourage further discussion by asking follow-up questions or inviting additional input from your commenters.
- **Show Appreciation:** Thank your followers for their comments and contributions to your posts.

Engaging with Other Users

1. Like and Comment on Posts

- **Active Participation:** Regularly like and comment on posts from your followers, industry peers, and influencers. This increases your visibility and fosters relationships.

- **Meaningful Comments:** Leave thoughtful comments that add value to the conversation rather than simple, generic comments.

2. Follow Relevant Accounts

- **Build Connections:** Follow accounts that are relevant to your niche or industry. Engaging with their content can attract their followers to your profile.
- **Networking:** Use Instagram as a networking tool to connect with industry leaders, potential collaborators, and your target audience.

Utilizing Instagram Stories

1. Share Daily Updates

- **Consistent Presence:** Use Stories to share daily updates, behind-the-scenes content, and time-sensitive information. This keeps your audience engaged between regular posts.

- **Variety:** Mix different types of content in your Stories, such as photos, videos, boomerangs, and GIFs, to keep them interesting.

2. Use Interactive Features

- **Polls and Quizzes:** Use polls and quizzes to engage your audience and gather feedback. These features make your Stories more interactive and engaging.
- **Questions:** Use the question sticker to invite your followers to ask you anything. Responding to these questions can foster deeper connections.

3. Highlight Important Stories

- **Save Key Stories:** Save important Stories in Highlight Reels on your profile. Highlights allow new followers to catch up on essential content and learn more about your brand.
- **Organize Highlights:** Create different Highlight categories, such as "Behind the Scenes," "Product Features," and "Customer Reviews," to make it easy for followers to find specific content.

Hosting Live Sessions

1. Plan Your Live Sessions

- **Schedule Regularly:** Host live sessions regularly to maintain consistent engagement. Announce the schedule in advance to ensure maximum attendance.
- **Prepare Content:** Plan the content and structure of your live sessions. Prepare talking points, questions, and any necessary materials in advance.

2. Engage in Real-Time

- **Real-Time Interaction:** Engage with viewers in real-time by responding to comments and questions during the live session. This makes the experience interactive and personal.
- **Acknowledge Viewers:** Acknowledge viewers by name and thank them for joining. This creates a sense of community and appreciation.

3. Collaborate with Guests

- **Invite Guests:** Collaborate with influencers, industry experts, or customers for joint live sessions. Guest appearances can attract their followers and provide diverse content.
- **Promote Collaborations:** Promote your live sessions with guests in advance to maximize attendance and engagement.

Encouraging User-Generated Content

1. Create a Branded Hashtag

- **Unique Hashtag:** Create a unique, branded hashtag that reflects your brand. Encourage your followers to use it when posting content related to your brand.
- **Promote the Hashtag:** Promote your branded hashtag in your bio, posts, and Stories to increase its visibility and usage.

2. Feature User Content

- Repost User-Generated Content: Share user-generated content on your profile and Stories. This not only provides you with additional content but also makes your followers feel appreciated and recognized.

- Credit Creators: Always credit the original creators when reposting their content. This builds trust and encourages more users to share their content with you.

3. Run Contests and Challenges

- Engagement Contests: Run contests that require followers to engage with your content, such as liking, commenting, or tagging friends.

- Challenges: Create and promote challenges that encourage followers to create and share content using your branded hashtag. For example, a fitness brand could create a #30DayFitnessChallenge.

Hosting Giveaways

1. Plan Your Giveaway

- Attractive Prizes: Offer prizes that are valuable and relevant to your audience. This increases participation and excitement.

- Simple Entry Requirements: Keep the entry requirements simple, such as liking a post, tagging friends, or following your account.

2. Promote Your Giveaway

- Visual Promotion: Use eye-catching graphics and videos to promote your giveaway across your feed, Stories, and other social media platforms.

- Collaborate with Influencers: Partner with influencers to promote your giveaway and reach a broader audience.

3. Announce Winners and Showcase Participation

- Public Announcement: Announce the winners publicly to maintain transparency and build trust.

- Highlight Entries: Showcase some of the best entries or user-generated content from participants.

This encourages future participation and builds community.

Engaging with Instagram's Features

1. Use IGTV and Reels

- Long-Form Content: Use IGTV for longer videos such as tutorials, interviews, or in-depth product reviews. This allows you to provide more value and engage your audience for longer periods.
- Short-Form Content: Use Reels to create short, engaging videos that can quickly capture attention and increase visibility. Participate in trending challenges and use popular music to reach a wider audience.

2. Utilize Polls and Questions

- Polls: Use polls in your Stories to gather opinions and feedback from your audience. This can provide valuable insights and make your followers feel involved.

- Questions: Use the question sticker in Stories to invite your followers to ask you anything or share their thoughts. Responding to these questions shows that you value their input and are approachable.

Building a Community

1. Foster a Sense of Belonging

- Community Building: Create a sense of community by engaging with your followers regularly and encouraging them to interact with each other.
- Inclusive Content: Share content that resonates with your audience's interests and values. Make your followers feel like they are part of a larger community.

2. Share Behind-the-Scenes Content

- Transparency: Share behind-the-scenes content to give your audience a glimpse into your brand's culture, processes, and people. This builds trust and authenticity.

- Exclusive Sneak Peeks: Provide sneak peeks of new products, upcoming events, or special projects to make your followers feel special and in the know.

3. Celebrate Milestones and Achievements

- Milestone Posts: Celebrate milestones such as reaching follower count goals, anniversaries, or significant achievements. Thank your followers for their support and make them feel part of your success.

- Highlight Community Achievements: Share stories of your followers' achievements or contributions to your community. This fosters a sense of belonging and mutual support.

By implementing these strategies, you can effectively engage with your Instagram audience, fostering a loyal and active community that supports your brand's growth. In the next chapter, we will explore advanced tactics for leveraging

Instagram analytics to optimize your marketing efforts.

Running Contests and Giveaways

Contests and giveaways are powerful tools for driving engagement, increasing your follower base, and promoting your products or services on Instagram. This chapter covers how to plan, promote, and execute successful contests and giveaways to maximize your reach and impact.

Planning Your Contest or Giveaway

1. Define Your Goals

- Increase Followers: Aim to boost your follower count by requiring participants to follow your account.
- Boost Engagement: Encourage likes, comments, and shares to increase interaction with your content.

- Promote Products: Use the contest to highlight a new product, service, or feature.

- Gather User-Generated Content: Encourage participants to create and share content related to your brand.

2. Choose an Enticing Prize

- Relevance: Select a prize that is relevant to your audience and brand. It should appeal to your target market.

- Value: Ensure the prize is valuable enough to motivate participation. High-value prizes tend to attract more participants.

3. Set Clear Entry Requirements

- Simple and Achievable: Keep the entry requirements simple and easy to achieve. Common requirements include following your account, liking a post, tagging friends, or sharing content using a specific hashtag.

- **Fair and Transparent:** Clearly outline the rules and eligibility criteria to avoid confusion and ensure fairness.

4. Establish a Timeline

- **Start and End Dates:** Set clear start and end dates for the contest or giveaway. Ensure the duration is long enough to allow ample participation but not so long that interest wanes.
- **Announcement Date:** Specify when and how the winner will be announced.

5. Create Engaging Visuals

- **Eye-Catching Graphics:** Design visually appealing graphics or videos to promote your contest. Use bold text, bright colors, and attractive images to capture attention.
- **Informative Content:** Include all necessary information in the visuals, such as the prize, entry requirements, and timeline.

Promoting Your Contest or Giveaway

1. Utilize Your Instagram Channels

- **Feed Posts:** Create multiple feed posts to announce and remind your audience about the contest. Use engaging visuals and compelling captions to draw attention.
- **Instagram Stories:** Use Stories to promote the contest daily. Utilize features like countdown stickers, polls, and swipe-up links (if applicable) to increase engagement.
- **IGTV and Reels:** Create short videos or tutorials explaining the contest details and promoting participation.

2. Leverage Other Social Media Platforms

- **Cross-Promotion:** Share the contest details on your other social media channels, such as Facebook, Twitter, and LinkedIn, to reach a broader audience.
- **Email Marketing:** Include information about the contest in your email newsletters to inform your existing subscribers.

3. Collaborate with Influencers and Partners

- **Influencer Promotions:** Partner with influencers who align with your brand to promote the contest to their followers. This can significantly increase your reach.
- **Brand Collaborations:** Collaborate with complementary brands for joint contests. This allows you to tap into each other's audience and offer more substantial prizes.

4. Encourage Sharing

- **Tag Friends:** Ask participants to tag their friends in the comments. This helps spread the word and brings in more participants.
- **Share to Stories:** Encourage participants to share the contest post or their entries to their Stories, increasing visibility.

Executing and Managing the Contest or Giveaway

1. Monitor Participation

- **Track Entries:** Keep track of all entries and ensure they meet the contest requirements. Use spreadsheets or contest management tools to organize and verify entries.
- **Engage with Participants:** Like and comment on participant entries to show appreciation and encourage further engagement.

2. Ensure Fairness and Transparency

- **Random Selection:** Use a random selection tool to pick the winner if your contest is based on chance. This ensures fairness and transparency.
- **Judging Criteria:** If the contest is based on skill or creativity, clearly outline the judging criteria and involve a panel of judges if necessary.

3. Announce the Winner

- **Public Announcement:** Announce the winner on your Instagram feed, Stories, and other platforms.

Use engaging visuals and celebrate the winner publicly.

- **Direct Contact:** Reach out to the winner via direct message or email to provide details on how they can claim their prize.

4. Follow Up

- **Post-Contest Content:** Share a post-contest update thanking all participants and showcasing some of the best entries. This helps maintain engagement and goodwill.
- **Feature the Winner:** Feature the winner on your profile and encourage them to share their experience with your product or service.

Measuring Success and Analyzing Results

1. Track Key Metrics

- **Follower Growth:** Measure the increase in your follower count during and after the contest.
- **Engagement Rates:** Track likes, comments, shares, and saves on your contest posts.

- Reach and Impressions: Analyze the reach and impressions of your contest posts to understand how many people saw your content.

2. Gather Feedback

- Participant Feedback: Ask participants for feedback on the contest experience. This can provide valuable insights for future contests.

- Internal Review: Conduct an internal review to assess what worked well and what could be improved for future contests.

3. Evaluate ROI

- Cost vs. Benefits: Compare the cost of running the contest (prizes, promotions, etc.) with the benefits gained (increased followers, engagement, sales, etc.).

- Conversion Rates: Analyze any increase in website traffic, sales, or leads generated from the contest participants.

By carefully planning, promoting, and managing your contests and giveaways, you can effectively engage your audience, attract new followers, and achieve your marketing goals. In the next chapter, we will explore advanced analytics and optimization techniques to further enhance your Instagram marketing strategy.

Collaborating with Influencers

Influencer collaborations offer a powerful way to expand your brand's reach, increase credibility, and drive engagement on Instagram. This chapter explores effective strategies for identifying, approaching, and collaborating with influencers to maximize the impact of your marketing efforts.

Identifying Relevant Influencers

1. Define Your Criteria

- **Relevance:** Look for influencers whose content aligns with your brand's niche, values, and target audience.

- **Engagement:** Prioritize influencers with high engagement rates, as this indicates an active and loyal follower base.

- **Reach:** Consider influencers with a significant following, but also evaluate the quality of their audience.

2. Use Influencer Marketing Tools

- **Social Listening Tools:** Use tools like BuzzSumo, Hootsuite, or Brandwatch to identify influencers who are already mentioning or engaging with your brand.

- **Influencer Platforms:** Explore influencer marketing platforms such as AspireIQ, Upfluence, or Influencity to discover and connect with relevant influencers.

3. Research Manually

- **Hashtag Searches:** Search relevant hashtags related to your industry or niche and identify influencers who regularly use them.

- **Explore Explore Page:** Browse the Explore page on Instagram to discover trending content and potential influencers in your niche.

Approaching Influencers

1. Personalize Your Outreach

- **Tailored Messages:** Craft personalized messages that demonstrate your understanding of the influencer's content and audience.

- **Highlight Benefits:** Clearly communicate the benefits of collaborating with your brand, such as exposure, product samples, or monetary compensation.

2. Be Transparent and Authentic

- **Disclosure:** Clearly outline your expectations, including compensation, deliverables, and any contractual agreements.

- **Authenticity:** Emphasize the authenticity of the collaboration and the value it can bring to both parties and their audiences.

3. Provide Creative Freedom

- **Collaborative Approach:** Involve influencers in the creative process and allow them creative freedom to produce content that resonates with their audience.
- **Guidelines:** Provide clear guidelines and brand messaging to ensure alignment with your brand's values and objectives.

Collaborative Content Strategies

1. Sponsored Posts

- **Product Reviews:** Have influencers create authentic reviews or testimonials featuring your products or services.
- **Promotional Campaigns:** Partner with influencers to promote specific campaigns, launches, or events related to your brand.

2. Takeovers and Day-in-the-Life

- **Instagram Takeovers:** Allow influencers to temporarily take over your brand's Instagram account to share behind-the-scenes content, Q&A sessions, or special announcements.
- **Day-in-the-Life:** Invite influencers to showcase a day in their life, incorporating your brand naturally into their activities.

3. Co-Created Content

- **Collaborative Projects:** Collaborate with influencers to co-create content such as videos, blog posts, or social media campaigns.
- **Giveaways and Contests:** Partner with influencers to host joint giveaways or contests, leveraging their audience to increase participation.

Managing Influencer Relationships

1. Communication

- Regular Updates: Maintain open and transparent communication throughout the collaboration process, providing regular updates on campaign progress and objectives.

- Feedback Loop: Encourage feedback from influencers to continuously improve collaboration strategies and content quality.

2. Compensation and Agreements

- Fair Compensation: Ensure fair compensation for influencers based on their reach, engagement, and scope of work.

- Contracts: Draft clear and comprehensive contracts outlining deliverables, timelines, payment terms, and any exclusivity agreements.

3. Performance Evaluation

- Analytics Tracking: Monitor key performance metrics such as engagement rates, follower growth, and website traffic generated by the influencer's content.

- **Feedback Surveys:** Collect feedback from influencers post-campaign to assess the collaboration's effectiveness and identify areas for improvement.

Leveraging Influencer Content

1. Repurpose Content

- **User-Generated Content:** Repurpose influencer-generated content for your own marketing channels, such as websites, email newsletters, or other social media platforms.
- **Testimonials and Reviews:** Incorporate influencer testimonials and reviews into your product pages or marketing materials to build credibility.

2. Extend Reach

- **Share Across Channels:** Amplify influencer content by sharing it across your brand's social media channels, website, and blog.

- Paid Promotion: Consider boosting influencer posts with paid promotion to extend their reach to a broader audience.

3. Build Long-Term Relationships

- Nurture Relationships: Cultivate long-term partnerships with influencers based on mutual trust, respect, and shared goals.
- Brand Ambassadors: Identify influencers who align closely with your brand values and mission, and explore opportunities for ongoing collaboration as brand ambassadors.

By following these strategies, you can effectively collaborate with influencers to elevate your brand's presence, connect with new audiences, and drive meaningful engagement on Instagram. In the next chapter, we will explore advanced tactics for analyzing and optimizing influencer campaigns for maximum impact.

Chapter 4: Advanced Marketing Strategies

As your Instagram marketing journey progresses, you'll want to delve into more advanced strategies to further enhance your brand's visibility, engagement, and ultimately, your bottom line. This chapter explores sophisticated tactics and techniques to take your Instagram marketing efforts to the next level.

Harnessing the Power of Instagram Analytics

1. Utilize Instagram Insights

- **Performance Metrics:** Dive deep into Instagram Insights to analyze key performance metrics such as reach, impressions, engagement, and follower demographics.
- **Content Analysis:** Identify top-performing posts, Stories, and IGTV videos to understand what resonates most with your audience.

- **Optimization Opportunities:** Use Insights data to refine your content strategy, posting schedule, and targeting tactics for better results.

2. Third-Party Analytics Tools

- **Comprehensive Analysis:** Leverage third-party analytics tools such as Sprout Social, Hootsuite Analytics, or Iconosquare for more in-depth analysis and reporting.
- **Competitor Benchmarking:** Compare your performance metrics with competitors and industry benchmarks to gain valuable insights and identify areas for improvement.
- **ROI Tracking:** Track the ROI of your Instagram marketing efforts by measuring metrics such as website traffic, conversions, and sales attributed to your Instagram activity.

Implementing Advanced Content Strategies

1. Interactive Content Formats

- **Polls and Quizzes:** Engage your audience with interactive content formats like polls, quizzes, and interactive sliders in Stories to encourage participation and gather feedback.

- **Shoppable Posts:** Utilize shoppable posts and product tags to make your Instagram feed more interactive and drive direct sales from your posts.

- **AR Filters and Effects:** Create custom AR filters and effects to enhance user engagement and brand awareness, leveraging Instagram's augmented reality features.

2. User-Generated Content Campaigns

- **UGC Contests:** Launch user-generated content (UGC) contests or challenges to encourage your followers to create and share content featuring your products or brand.

- **UGC Repurposing:** Repurpose UGC across your marketing channels to build trust, authenticity, and social proof, showcasing real customers using and enjoying your products.

- Influencer Partnerships: Collaborate with influencers to amplify UGC campaigns and reach a wider audience through their networks.

Mastering Instagram Advertising

1. Advanced Targeting Options

- Custom Audiences: Create custom audience segments based on specific criteria such as website visitors, email subscribers, or previous customers for more targeted ad campaigns.
- Lookalike Audiences: Expand your reach by targeting lookalike audiences that share similarities with your existing customers, increasing the likelihood of reaching potential new customers.

2. Dynamic Ads and Retargeting

- Dynamic Product Ads: Automatically promote relevant products to users based on their browsing behavior or past interactions with your website or app.

- **Retargeting Campaigns:** Retarget users who have interacted with your brand but haven't completed a desired action (e.g., making a purchase) with personalized ads to encourage conversion.

Leveraging Influencer Marketing at Scale

1. Macro and Mega Influencers

- **Macro Influencers:** Partner with macro influencers who have a larger following and reach but still maintain high levels of engagement with their audience.
- **Mega Influencers:** Collaborate with mega influencers, celebrities, or industry leaders to reach massive audiences and generate buzz around your brand or product launches.

2. Affiliate Marketing Programs

- **Affiliate Partnerships:** Establish affiliate marketing programs with influencers, where they earn a commission for driving sales or conversions through their unique affiliate links.

- Performance-Based Compensation: Incentivize influencers to promote your products or services by offering performance-based compensation tied to the results they deliver.

Scaling Your Instagram Presence

1. Cross-Platform Integration

- Omni-Channel Marketing: Integrate your Instagram marketing efforts with other marketing channels such as Facebook, Twitter, Pinterest, and TikTok to reach audiences across multiple platforms.

- Unified Brand Messaging: Maintain consistency in brand messaging, visual identity, and content strategy across all marketing channels for a cohesive brand experience.

2. Automation and Efficiency Tools

- Social Media Management Platforms: Use social media management tools like Buffer, Later, or Sprout Social to schedule posts, track performance, and manage multiple accounts more efficiently.

Embracing Emerging Trends and Features

1. Video Content Dominance

- Short-Form Video: Embrace the rise of short-form video content formats like Instagram Reels and leverage their popularity to increase engagement and reach on the platform.
- Live Video: Host live Q&A sessions, behind-the-scenes tours, product demonstrations, and interactive workshops to connect with your audience in real-time and foster meaningful interactions.

2. Ephemeral Content

- Fleeting Content: Embrace ephemeral content formats like Instagram Stories and leverage their

temporary nature to create a sense of urgency, exclusivity, and FOMO (fear of missing out) among your audience.

- Story Highlights: Curate and organize your best-performing Stories into Highlights on your profile to showcase your brand's story, products, and value proposition to new visitors.

By incorporating these advanced marketing strategies into your Instagram marketing playbook, you can elevate your brand's presence, drive meaningful engagement, and achieve your business objectives more effectively on the platform. Experiment, analyze, and iterate to find the strategies that work best for your brand and audience.

Instagram Advertising: A Comprehensive Guide

Instagram advertising offers businesses a powerful way to reach a highly engaged audience and achieve various marketing objectives. This chapter provides a comprehensive guide to creating,

managing, and optimizing Instagram ad campaigns to maximize your return on investment (ROI).

Understanding Instagram Ad Formats

1. Photo Ads

- **Visual Appeal:** Utilize high-quality images to capture attention and convey your message effectively.
- **Simplicity:** Keep your design clean and focused to ensure your call-to-action (CTA) stands out.

2. Video Ads

- **Engagement:** Leverage videos to showcase products, tell stories, or demonstrate features in an engaging way.
- **Length:** Keep videos concise (15-60 seconds) to maintain viewer interest.

3. Carousel Ads

- **Multiple Images/Videos:** Include multiple images or videos in a single ad to highlight different products, features, or benefits.
- **Interactive Experience:** Encourage users to swipe through the carousel for a more interactive experience.

4. Stories Ads

- **Full-Screen Experience:** Take advantage of the immersive full-screen format of Instagram Stories.
- **Ephemeral Content:** Use the temporary nature of Stories to create urgency and drive immediate action.

5. Collection Ads

- **Product Catalog:** Showcase a collection of products directly within the ad, allowing users to browse and shop seamlessly.
- **Immersive Experience:** Combine video or images with product images to create an engaging shopping experience.

6. Explore Ads

- **Discoverability:** Place ads within the Explore feed to reach users who are actively looking for new content.
- **Targeting:** Leverage Instagram's targeting options to reach a broader audience interested in similar content.

7. Shopping Ads

- **Shoppable Posts:** Tag products directly in your ads to allow users to purchase without leaving the app.
- **Seamless Integration:** Integrate your product catalog with Instagram for a streamlined shopping experience.

Setting Up Your Instagram Ad Campaign

1. Define Your Objectives

- **Awareness:** Increase brand visibility and reach a larger audience.

- Consideration: Drive traffic to your website, generate leads, or encourage app installs.

- Conversions: Increase sales, sign-ups, or other specific actions on your website or app.

2. Choose Your Target Audience

- Demographics: Target based on age, gender, location, and language.

- Interests: Reach users based on their interests, behaviors, and activities on Instagram and Facebook.

- Custom Audiences: Use your existing customer data to create custom audiences.

- Lookalike Audiences: Reach new users similar to your best customers by creating lookalike audiences.

3. Set Your Budget and Schedule

- Budget Types: Choose between daily budget (spend a specific amount per day) or lifetime budget (spend a total amount over the campaign's duration).

- Ad Schedule: Determine the start and end dates for your campaign, and choose whether to run ads continuously or on a specific schedule.

4. Design Your Ads

- Visuals: Use high-quality images or videos that align with your brand and campaign objectives.

- Copy: Write compelling ad copy that includes a clear call-to-action (CTA) to guide users on what to do next.

- CTA Buttons: Choose from various CTA buttons such as "Shop Now," "Learn More," or "Sign Up" to match your campaign goals.

5. Launch Your Campaign

- Review and Publish: Double-check all elements of your campaign, including targeting, budget, and creatives, before publishing.

- Monitor Performance: Use Instagram Insights and Ads Manager to track your campaign's performance and make adjustments as needed.

Optimizing Your Instagram Ad Campaign

1. A/B Testing

- **Test Variations:** Create multiple versions of your ads to test different images, videos, copy, and CTAs.
- **Analyze Results:** Compare the performance of each variation to determine what resonates best with your audience.

2. Monitor Key Metrics

- **Impressions and Reach:** Track how many people see your ads and how often.
- **Engagement:** Measure likes, comments, shares, and saves to gauge user interaction.
- **Click-Through Rate (CTR):** Analyze the percentage of users who click on your ad.
- **Conversion Rate:** Track the percentage of users who complete a desired action after clicking your ad.

3. Adjust Targeting

- **Refine Audiences:** Use performance data to refine your audience targeting, focusing on demographics and interests that yield the best results.
- **Exclude Audiences:** Exclude users who have already converted or are unlikely to be interested in your offer to optimize your ad spend.

4. Optimize Ad Creatives

- **Update Visuals:** Regularly refresh your ad visuals to prevent ad fatigue and maintain user interest.
- **Refine Copy:** Continuously test and refine your ad copy to improve clarity, relevance, and effectiveness.

5. Budget Allocation

- **Reallocate Budget:** Shift your budget towards high-performing ads and audiences to maximize ROI.

- Scale Successful Campaigns: Increase your budget for campaigns that consistently deliver strong results.

Advanced Strategies for Instagram Advertising

1. Retargeting Campaigns

- Website Visitors: Retarget users who have visited your website but did not convert with personalized ads to encourage them to complete their purchase.

- Engaged Users: Retarget users who have engaged with your Instagram content (likes, comments, shares) to drive them further down the conversion funnel.

2. Dynamic Ads

- Personalized Ads: Use dynamic ads to automatically show the most relevant products to users based on their past behavior and interests.

- **Catalog Integration:** Integrate your product catalog with Instagram to enable dynamic ads and ensure your ad content is always up-to-date.

3. Influencer-Driven Ads

- **Influencer Partnerships:** Collaborate with influencers to create authentic and engaging ad content that resonates with their followers.
- **Boosted Posts:** Amplify influencer-created content by turning it into ads to reach a larger audience and drive more engagement.

4. Sequential Advertising

- **Storytelling:** Use sequential ads to tell a cohesive brand story or guide users through a step-by-step journey.
- **Multiple Touchpoints:** Create a series of ads that progressively educate, engage, and convert users over time.

5. Geo-Targeting

- Local Promotions: Use geo-targeting to reach users in specific locations with localized promotions and offers.

- Event Targeting: Target users in the vicinity of specific events or landmarks to capitalize on local traffic and interest.

By implementing these advanced strategies and continuously optimizing your campaigns, you can effectively leverage Instagram advertising to drive significant business results. Stay informed about the latest features and trends on the platform to ensure your campaigns remain relevant and impactful.

Utilizing Instagram Shopping

Instagram Shopping transforms your profile into a digital storefront, making it easy for users to browse and purchase products directly from your posts and Stories. This chapter provides a step-by-step guide to setting up and optimizing Instagram Shopping to drive sales and enhance the shopping experience for your customers.

Setting Up Instagram Shopping

1. Ensure Eligibility

- **Business Account:** You must have an Instagram business account.
- **Supported Markets:** Ensure your business is located in a supported market for Instagram Shopping.
- **Product Eligibility:** Only physical goods are eligible for Instagram Shopping.

2. Connect Your Facebook Catalog

- **Facebook Shop:** Create a Facebook Shop and connect your Instagram business account.
- **Catalog Manager:** Use Facebook Catalog Manager or an e-commerce platform partner (like Shopify or BigCommerce) to manage your product catalog.

3. Submit Your Account for Review

- **Account Review:** Once your product catalog is connected, submit your account for review in the Instagram app (Settings > Business > Set Up Instagram Shopping).
- **Approval:** Instagram will notify you once your account is approved, allowing you to start tagging products in your posts and Stories.

Setting Up Your Shop

1. Create Product Listings

- **High-Quality Images:** Use high-quality images that accurately represent your products.
- **Detailed Descriptions:** Include detailed product descriptions, prices, and relevant information to help customers make informed decisions.
- **Consistent Branding:** Ensure your product listings align with your brand's visual identity and tone of voice.

2. Organize Your Shop

- **Collections:** Group related products into collections (e.g., "New Arrivals," "Best Sellers," "Summer Collection") to make it easier for users to browse.

- **Customization:** Customize your Shop's layout and style to reflect your brand's aesthetic.

3. Optimize Your Shop

- **SEO-Friendly Descriptions:** Use keywords in your product descriptions to improve search visibility within Instagram Shopping.

- **Tags and Categories:** Use relevant tags and categories to help users discover your products more easily.

Tagging Products in Posts and Stories

1. Tagging in Feed Posts

- **Single Image or Video:** Tag up to five products per image or video post.

- **Carousel Posts:** Tag up to 20 products in carousel posts (up to five products per image or video).

2. Tagging in Stories

- **Product Stickers:** Use product stickers to tag products in your Stories. Users can tap the sticker to view product details and make a purchase.
- **Swipe Up Links:** If you have over 10,000 followers or a verified account, use the swipe-up feature to link directly to product pages.

3. Using Product Tags Effectively

- **Natural Integration:** Integrate product tags naturally within your posts and Stories, ensuring they enhance rather than detract from the content.
- **Multiple Angles:** Show products from multiple angles and in different contexts to give users a comprehensive view.

Promoting Your Shop

1. Highlighting Products in Your Bio

- **Shop Link:** Include a direct link to your Shop in your Instagram bio.
- **Call to Action:** Use a compelling call to action (e.g., "Shop our latest collection!") to encourage users to visit your Shop.

2. Utilizing Instagram Ads

- **Shoppable Ads:** Create shoppable ads that include product tags, allowing users to purchase directly from the ad.
- **Dynamic Ads:** Use dynamic ads to show personalized product recommendations based on user behavior.

3. Collaborating with Influencers

- **Influencer Partnerships:** Partner with influencers to showcase your products in authentic and engaging ways.

- Product Placements: Feature your products in influencer content, utilizing their reach to drive traffic to your Shop.

Enhancing the Shopping Experience

1. Streamlined Checkout

- In-App Checkout: Enable Instagram's in-app checkout feature (available in select markets) to allow users to complete purchases without leaving the app.
- Smooth Process: Ensure a smooth and intuitive checkout process, minimizing steps and reducing friction.

2. Customer Reviews and UGC

- Customer Reviews: Encourage customers to leave reviews and share their experiences with your products.
- User-Generated Content: Showcase user-generated content (UGC) featuring your products to build trust and authenticity.

3. Customer Support

- **Responsive Support:** Provide prompt and helpful customer support to address any issues or inquiries.
- **FAQs:** Include a FAQ section in your Shop to answer common questions and provide additional information.

Analyzing and Optimizing Performance

1. Tracking Metrics

- **Insights:** Use Instagram Insights to track key metrics such as product views, clicks, and purchases.
- **Sales Data:** Analyze sales data to identify top-performing products and trends.

2. A/B Testing

- **Content Testing:** Conduct A/B tests on different types of content, product tags, and CTAs to determine what drives the most engagement and sales.

- Audience Segmentation: Test different audience segments to optimize targeting and improve conversion rates.

3. Continuous Improvement

- Feedback Loop: Gather feedback from customers and use it to make continuous improvements to your Shop and product offerings.

- Stay Updated: Stay updated with Instagram's latest features and trends to ensure your Shop remains competitive and relevant.

By effectively utilizing Instagram Shopping, you can create a seamless and engaging shopping experience for your customers, drive sales, and grow your business on the platform. Implement these strategies to maximize the potential of Instagram Shopping and transform your profile into a powerful sales channel.

Analytics and Insights: Measuring Your Success

Understanding the impact of your Instagram marketing efforts is crucial for optimizing your strategy and achieving your business goals. This chapter delves into the key metrics and tools for measuring success on Instagram, enabling you to make data-driven decisions and continuously improve your performance.

Key Instagram Metrics to Track

1. Engagement Metrics

- **Likes:** Measure the number of likes on your posts to gauge initial reactions and content popularity.
- **Comments:** Track comments to assess user interaction and engagement with your content.
- **Shares:** Monitor the number of times your content is shared to understand its reach and virality.
- **Saves:** Evaluate saves as an indicator of valuable and bookmark-worthy content.

2. Reach and Impressions

- **Reach:** Track the number of unique users who have seen your content. This helps you understand your content's exposure and audience size.
- **Impressions:** Measure the total number of times your content has been viewed, including multiple views by the same user.

3. Follower Growth

- **New Followers:** Monitor the number of new followers gained over a specific period to evaluate your growth rate.
- **Unfollowers:** Track the number of users who unfollow your account to identify potential issues or content that might be driving users away.

4. Profile Interactions

- **Profile Visits:** Measure the number of visits to your profile, indicating interest in your brand.

- **Website Clicks:** Track clicks on the link in your bio to assess the effectiveness of driving traffic to your website.

- **Email and Call Clicks:** Monitor the number of users clicking on contact options (email, call) to evaluate user intent for direct interaction.

5. Instagram Stories Metrics

- **Views:** Measure the number of views on your Stories to gauge their reach.

- **Replies:** Track replies to your Stories to understand user engagement and feedback.

- **Exits:** Monitor the number of exits to identify where users lose interest and leave your Story.

6. Shopping Metrics

- **Product Views:** Track the number of views on product tags in your Shopping posts.

- **Clicks on Product Tags:** Measure clicks on product tags to assess interest in specific products.

- Purchases: Monitor the number of purchases made directly through Instagram Shopping to evaluate sales performance.

Utilizing Instagram Insights

1. Accessing Instagram Insights

- Business Account: Ensure you have an Instagram business account to access Instagram Insights.
- Insights Dashboard: Navigate to the Insights dashboard from your profile (tap the menu icon and select Insights).

2. Overview of Insights Sections

- Content: Analyze the performance of your posts, Stories, and promotions.
- Activity: Track actions taken on your account, including profile visits, website clicks, and interactions.

- **Audience:** Understand your audience demographics, including age, gender, location, and active times.

3. Content Insights

- **Top Posts:** Identify your top-performing posts based on engagement, reach, and impressions.
- **Stories Performance:** Evaluate the performance of your Stories, including views, replies, and exits.
- **IGTV and Reels:** Track the performance of IGTV videos and Reels, including views, likes, comments, and shares.

4. Activity Insights

- **Interactions:** Measure the total interactions on your account, such as profile visits, website clicks, and email/call clicks.
- **Discovery:** Understand how users are discovering your content through reach, impressions, and sources (e.g., Explore page, hashtags).

5. Audience Insights

- **Follower Demographics:** Analyze the age, gender, and location of your followers to tailor your content strategy.
- **Active Times:** Identify the days and times when your followers are most active to optimize your posting schedule.

Third-Party Analytics Tools

1. Comprehensive Analysis

- **Sprout Social:** Use Sprout Social to gain detailed insights into your Instagram performance, including engagement, reach, and follower growth.
- **Hootsuite Analytics:** Leverage Hootsuite Analytics for in-depth reporting and analysis of your Instagram metrics.
- **Iconosquare:** Utilize Iconosquare for advanced Instagram analytics, including competitor benchmarking and content performance tracking.

2. Competitor Benchmarking

- **Competitive Insights:** Compare your performance with competitors to identify strengths and areas for improvement.

- **Industry Benchmarks:** Use industry benchmarks to set realistic performance goals and measure your success against peers.

3. ROI Tracking

- **Conversion Metrics:** Track conversion metrics such as website visits, lead generation, and sales attributed to Instagram marketing efforts.

- **Campaign Performance:** Evaluate the ROI of specific campaigns to understand their impact on your business objectives.

A/B Testing and Experimentation

1. Creating Test Variations

- **Ad Creatives:** Test different images, videos, and ad copy to identify the most effective creative elements.

- **Post Formats:** Experiment with various post formats (e.g., carousel posts, videos, Stories) to determine what resonates best with your audience.

2. Analyzing Test Results

- **Performance Comparison:** Compare the performance of different test variations to identify the best-performing elements.
- **Data-Driven Decisions:** Use test results to make informed decisions and optimize your content and ad strategy.

3. Continuous Improvement

- **Iterative Testing:** Continuously test and refine your content and ad strategies to stay ahead of trends and maintain engagement.
- **Feedback Loop:** Incorporate user feedback and performance data to improve future campaigns and content.

Optimizing Your Instagram Strategy

1. Data-Driven Strategy

- **Performance Analysis:** Regularly analyze your performance metrics to identify trends, strengths, and areas for improvement.
- **Strategy Adjustments:** Use insights to make data-driven adjustments to your content strategy, posting schedule, and targeting.

2. Audience Engagement

- **Interactive Content:** Create interactive content such as polls, quizzes, and Q&A sessions to boost engagement.
- **Community Building:** Foster a sense of community by responding to comments, engaging with followers, and encouraging user-generated content.

3. Trend Monitoring

- **Stay Updated:** Keep up with the latest Instagram trends, features, and best practices to ensure your strategy remains relevant.

- Innovative Approaches: Experiment with new content formats and innovative approaches to keep your audience engaged and attract new followers.

By effectively utilizing analytics and insights, you can measure your success on Instagram, optimize your strategy, and achieve your marketing objectives. Continuously analyze your performance, experiment with new tactics, and stay informed about the latest trends to maintain a competitive edge on the platform.

A/B Testing and Optimizing Your Campaigns

A/B testing is a crucial process for optimizing your Instagram marketing campaigns. By systematically testing different elements of your ads and content, you can determine what resonates best with your audience and make data-driven decisions to enhance your overall strategy. This chapter will guide you through the steps of setting up, conducting, and analyzing A/B tests, and offer tips for continuous optimization.

Setting Up A/B Tests

1. Define Your Objectives

- **Clear Goals:** Establish clear objectives for your A/B tests. Are you trying to increase engagement, drive more traffic, boost conversions, or improve brand awareness?
- **Key Metrics:** Identify the key metrics that will measure the success of your tests. These could include click-through rates (CTR), conversion rates, engagement rates, and more.

2. Select Variables to Test

- **Ad Creatives:** Test different images, videos, and design elements to see which visuals capture the most attention.
- **Copy and Headlines:** Experiment with variations in ad copy and headlines to identify the most compelling messages.

- **Random Audience:** Ensure that your audience is randomly split between the control and variant groups to avoid bias.

- **Sample Size:** Use a sufficiently large sample size to ensure that your test results are statistically significant.

2. Running the Test

- **Equal Exposure:** Run the test for a sufficient period to gather enough data, ensuring both the control and variant receive equal exposure.

- **Monitor Performance:** Regularly monitor the performance of your tests to ensure they are running smoothly and gathering data effectively.

3. Analyzing Test Results

1. Key Metrics Analysis

- **CTR (Click-Through Rate):** Measure the percentage of users who clicked on your ad or post to assess its attractiveness.

- **Conversion Rate:** Track the percentage of users who completed a desired action (e.g., purchase, sign-up) to evaluate the effectiveness of your content.
- **Engagement Rate:** Analyze the level of engagement (likes, comments, shares) to determine how well your content resonates with your audience.

2. Statistical Significance

- **Confidence Level:** Use a statistical confidence level (typically 95%) to determine if your test results are significant and not due to random chance.
- **P-Value:** Calculate the p-value to assess the probability that the observed differences between the control and variant are significant.

3. Interpreting Results

- **Winning Variation:** Identify the winning variation based on the key metrics and statistical significance.

- Insights and Learnings: Gather insights from the test results to understand what elements contributed to the success or failure of each variation.

Optimizing Your Campaigns

1. Implementing Changes

- Adopt Winning Variations: Implement the winning variations from your A/B tests into your ongoing campaigns.

- Iterative Improvements: Use the insights from your tests to make iterative improvements to your ad creatives, copy, targeting, and overall strategy.

2. Continuous Testing

- Regular Testing: Continuously conduct A/B tests to keep your campaigns optimized and up-to-date with changing audience preferences.

- New Variables: Regularly introduce new variables to test (e.g., new ad formats, different messaging) to keep your strategy innovative.

3. Monitoring Performance

- **Ongoing Analysis:** Regularly monitor the performance of your optimized campaigns to ensure they continue to deliver strong results.
- **Adjust and Adapt:** Be prepared to make adjustments based on performance data and new insights from ongoing tests.

4. Leveraging Automation Tools

- **Ad Optimization Tools:** Use automation tools like Facebook Ads Manager's A/B Testing feature or third-party tools to streamline your testing process.
- **Performance Tracking Tools:** Leverage analytics tools to track performance metrics and gather insights efficiently.

Best Practices for A/B Testing

1. Hypothesis-Driven Testing

- **Formulate Hypotheses:** Develop clear hypotheses for each test to understand what you aim to learn or achieve.
- **Test Rationale:** Ensure each test has a strong rationale and is based on data-driven insights or observed patterns.

2. Focus on One Variable at a Time

- **Isolate Variables:** Change only one variable per test to isolate its impact and gain clear insights.
- **Sequential Testing:** Conduct sequential tests to explore the impact of multiple variables over time.

3. Maintain Consistency

- **Consistent Conditions:** Ensure that external factors (e.g., ad budget, target audience size) remain consistent across the test period.
- **Test Duration:** Run tests for a sufficient duration to gather reliable data, typically at least 7-14 days.

4. Learn from Failures

- **Analyze Unsuccessful Tests:** Understand why certain variations didn't perform well to avoid similar mistakes in the future.

- **Iterate Based on Insights:** Use insights from unsuccessful tests to inform future tests and drive continuous improvement.

5. Document and Share Findings

- **Record Results:** Document the results and insights from each test to build a knowledge base for your team.

- **Share Learnings:** Share key findings with your team to foster a culture of data-driven decision-making and collaborative improvement.

By systematically conducting A/B tests and leveraging the insights gained, you can continuously optimize your Instagram marketing campaigns, enhance engagement, and drive better business results. Remember to stay agile and adaptive, as the digital landscape and audience preferences are constantly evolving.

Leveraging Instagram Features for Maximum Impact

Instagram offers a rich array of features designed to help businesses connect with their audience, showcase their brand, and drive engagement. This chapter explores how to effectively use these features to maximize your impact on the platform.

Instagram Feed Posts

1. High-Quality Visuals

- **Professional Photos:** Use high-resolution, professionally-shot photos to capture attention.
- **Consistent Aesthetic:** Maintain a consistent visual style and color palette to create a cohesive brand identity.
- **Engaging Captions:** Write compelling captions that complement your visuals and encourage interaction.

2. Carousel Posts

- **Multiple Images/Videos:** Use carousel posts to showcase multiple images or videos in a single post.

- **Storytelling:** Tell a story or provide a step-by-step guide using a series of related images.

- **Product Showcase:** Highlight different features or uses of a product in each slide.

Instagram Stories

1. Daily Updates

- **Behind-the-Scenes:** Share behind-the-scenes content to give your audience a glimpse into your brand's daily operations.

- **Product Demos:** Create short, engaging product demos to highlight features and benefits.

- **Event Coverage:** Use Stories to provide live updates from events or special occasions.

2. Interactive Features

- **Polls and Questions:** Use polls, questions, and quizzes to engage your audience and gather feedback.
- **Swipe-Up Links:** If eligible, use the swipe-up feature to direct followers to your website, product pages, or other external links.
- **Countdowns:** Create excitement and anticipation for upcoming events or product launches with countdown stickers.

Instagram Reels

1. Short, Engaging Videos

- **Creative Content****: Produce creative, entertaining, and engaging short videos that capture your audience's attention.
- **Trends and Challenges:** Participate in trending challenges or create your own to boost visibility and engagement.
- **Educational Content:** Share quick tips, tutorials, or how-to videos to provide value to your audience.

2. Music and Effects

- **Popular Music:** Use popular music tracks to enhance your Reels and make them more engaging.
- **Special Effects:** Utilize Instagram's effects and filters to add a creative touch to your videos.

Instagram IGTV

1. Long-Form Videos

- **In-Depth Content:** Share longer, more in-depth videos on topics relevant to your audience.
- **Interviews and Webinars:** Post interviews, webinars, or panel discussions to provide valuable insights and information.
- **Product Reviews:** Create detailed product reviews or unboxing videos to showcase your offerings.

2. Series Content

- **Regular Series:** Develop a regular series of videos to keep your audience coming back for more.
- **Consistent Branding:** Maintain consistent branding elements (e.g., intro/outro, color schemes) across all IGTV videos.

Instagram Live

1. Real-Time Engagement

- **Live Q&A:** Host live Q&A sessions to interact directly with your audience and answer their questions.
- **Product Launches:** Use Instagram Live to announce and demonstrate new products in real time.
- **Collaborations:** Partner with influencers or industry experts for live discussions, interviews, or joint events.

2. Promote and Save

- Promotion: Promote your upcoming live sessions through Stories, feed posts, and countdown stickers.

- Save to IGTV: Save your live sessions to IGTV so followers can watch them later if they missed the live broadcast.

Instagram Shopping

1. Product Tags

- Tag Products: Use product tags in your feed posts and Stories to link directly to product pages.

- Seamless Shopping: Provide a seamless shopping experience by allowing users to purchase directly from your posts.

2. Shopping Ads

- Promote Products: Use shopping ads to promote your products to a wider audience and drive sales.

- **Dynamic Ads:** Create dynamic ads that automatically show products based on user interests and behavior.

Instagram Guides

1. Curated Content

- **Resource Collections:** Curate collections of posts, products, or places to provide valuable resources for your audience.
- **Thematic Guides:** Create guides around specific themes, such as holiday gift guides, travel tips, or fitness routines.

2. Expert Recommendations

- **Expert Tips:** Share expert tips and recommendations to position your brand as a thought leader in your industry.
- **Collaborate:** Collaborate with influencers or experts to create co-branded guides.

Analytics and Insights

1. Monitor Performance

- **Instagram Insights:** Use Instagram Insights to track the performance of your posts, Stories, Reels, and IGTV videos.
- **Engagement Metrics:** Monitor key engagement metrics such as likes, comments, shares, and saves to understand what content resonates with your audience.

2. Adjust Strategy

- **Data-Driven Decisions:** Use the insights gathered to make data-driven decisions and adjust your content strategy accordingly.
- **Continuous Improvement:** Regularly review and analyze your performance data to identify areas for improvement and optimize your efforts.

Tips for Maximizing Impact

1. Consistency is Key

- **Regular Posting:** Maintain a consistent posting schedule to keep your audience engaged and attract new followers.
- **Brand Voice:** Develop and maintain a consistent brand voice across all your content.

2. Engage with Your Audience

- **Respond to Comments:** Actively respond to comments and messages to foster a sense of community and build relationships.
- **Encourage Interaction:** Use interactive features like polls, questions, and quizzes to encourage audience participation.

3. Stay Updated with Trends

- **Follow Trends:** Keep an eye on current trends and incorporate them into your content to stay relevant and engage your audience.
- **Innovate:** Don't be afraid to experiment with new features and content formats to find what works best for your brand.

- Call-to-Action (CTA): Test different CTAs (e.g., "Shop Now," "Learn More," "Sign Up") to find out which one drives the most action.

- Target Audiences: Test different audience segments based on demographics, interests, and behaviors to determine which groups respond best to your content.

- Post Timing: Experiment with posting at different times of the day or week to see when your audience is most active.

3. Create Test Variations

- Control and Variant: For each A/B test, create a control (original) version and one or more variant versions with the changes you want to test.

- Consistent Variables: Ensure that only one variable is changed between the control and variant to isolate the impact of that specific element.

Conducting A/B Tests

1. Randomization

By leveraging Instagram's diverse features effectively, you can enhance your brand's presence on the platform, engage with your audience in meaningful ways, and drive significant business results. Implement these strategies to maximize your impact and achieve your marketing goals on Instagram.

Chapter 5: Turning Followers into Customers

Turning your Instagram followers into customers is the ultimate goal of any marketing strategy on the platform. While building a large and engaged following is crucial, converting those followers into paying customers requires strategic planning and execution. This chapter explores the techniques and tactics to transform your Instagram audience into loyal customers, driving sales and boosting your business growth.

Understanding Your Customer Journey

1. Awareness Stage

- **Attract Attention:** Use visually appealing and engaging content to attract potential customers. Focus on high-quality images, videos, and captivating captions.

- **Brand Storytelling:** Share your brand's story to create a personal connection with your audience. Highlight your values, mission, and unique selling points.

2. Consideration Stage

- **Educational Content:** Provide valuable information and educate your audience about your products or services. Use tutorials, how-to guides, and product demonstrations.
- **Customer Testimonials:** Share testimonials and reviews from satisfied customers to build trust and credibility.

3. Decision Stage

- **Promotions and Discounts:** Offer exclusive promotions, discounts, and limited-time offers to encourage followers to make a purchase.
- **Clear CTAs:** Use clear and compelling calls-to-action (CTAs) in your posts and stories to guide followers towards making a purchase.

Optimizing Your Instagram Profile for Conversions

1. Business Profile

- **Professional Appearance:** Ensure your profile looks professional and trustworthy. Use a high-quality profile picture, preferably your brand logo.
- **Bio Optimization:** Craft a concise and compelling bio that clearly communicates your value proposition and includes a strong CTA.
- **Contact Information:** Provide clear contact information, including email, phone number, and address if applicable, to make it easy for followers to reach you.

2. Link in Bio

- **Link Tree Tools:** Use tools like <u>Linktree</u> or <u>Lnk.Bio</u> to create a single link that directs followers to multiple destinations, such as your website, blog, or product pages.
- **Landing Pages:** Create dedicated landing pages for Instagram traffic to provide a seamless user

experience and increase the likelihood of conversions.

Content Strategies for Conversion

1. Shoppable Posts and Stories

- **Product Tags:** Use Instagram's shopping features to tag products in your posts and stories, allowing followers to shop directly from your content.
- **Shopping Stickers:** Add shopping stickers to your stories to make it easy for followers to view product details and make purchases.

2. User-Generated Content (UGC)

- **Encourage UGC:** Encourage your followers to share their experiences with your products by creating a branded hashtag and featuring UGC on your profile.
- **Leverage Social Proof:** Share UGC in your posts and stories to showcase real-life usage and satisfaction, enhancing credibility and trust.

3. Influencer Collaborations

- **Partner with Influencers:** Collaborate with influencers who align with your brand and have a loyal following. Their endorsement can significantly boost your credibility and reach.
- **Sponsored Content:** Use sponsored posts and stories to reach new audiences and drive traffic to your profile and website.

Engaging Your Audience to Drive Sales

1. Interactive Stories

- **Polls and Quizzes:** Use interactive features like polls, quizzes, and questions to engage your audience and gather feedback.
- **Countdown Stickers:** Create excitement for upcoming product launches or promotions with countdown stickers in your stories.

2. Live Sessions

- **Live Q&A:** Host live Q&A sessions to address customer queries, provide product insights, and create a sense of community.

- **Live Product Demos:** Conduct live demonstrations of your products to showcase their features and benefits in real-time.

Utilizing Instagram Ads for Conversions

1. Targeted Ads

- **Audience Segmentation:** Use Instagram's advanced targeting options to reach specific audience segments based on demographics, interests, and behaviors.

- **Retargeting Campaigns:** Implement retargeting campaigns to reach users who have interacted with your content but haven't made a purchase yet.

2. Ad Formats

- **Carousel Ads:** Use carousel ads to showcase multiple products or highlight different features of a single product.

- Video Ads: Leverage the power of video ads to provide a more immersive and engaging experience for your audience.

Tracking and Analyzing Performance

1. Analytics Tools

- Instagram Insights: Utilize Instagram Insights to track key metrics such as engagement rates, click-through rates, and conversion rates.
- Third-Party Analytics: Use third-party analytics tools for more in-depth analysis and reporting.

2. Key Metrics

- Engagement Rate: Monitor the engagement rate of your posts and stories to gauge audience interest and interaction.
- Click-Through Rate (CTR): Track the CTR of your links in bio, posts, and stories to measure the effectiveness of your CTAs.

- **Conversion Rate:** Measure the conversion rate of your shoppable posts, ads, and landing pages to evaluate the success of your efforts.

Building Customer Loyalty

1. Post-Purchase Engagement

- **Thank You Messages:** Send personalized thank you messages to customers who make a purchase.
- **Customer Support:** Provide excellent customer support through direct messages and comments to address any issues or questions.

2. Loyalty Programs

- **Exclusive Offers:** Offer exclusive discounts, early access to new products, and special promotions to loyal customers.
- **Reward Programs:** Implement a reward program to incentivize repeat purchases and long-term loyalty.

3. Continuous Feedback

- **Surveys and Feedback Forms****: Use surveys and feedback forms to gather customer insights and improve your products and services.

- **Adapt and Improve:** Continuously adapt and improve your strategies based on customer feedback and performance data.

By strategically leveraging Instagram's features and implementing these tactics, you can effectively turn your followers into loyal customers. Focus on providing value, building trust, and creating a seamless shopping experience to drive conversions and grow your business on Instagram.

Developing a Sales Funnel on Instagram

Creating an effective sales funnel on Instagram is crucial for guiding your followers through the buyer's journey, transforming casual browsers into loyal customers. This chapter will walk you through the steps to build a robust sales funnel, utilizing

Instagram's features and content strategies to maximize conversions and drive business growth.

Understanding the Sales Funnel Stages

1. Awareness
- **Goal:** Capture the attention of potential customers.
- **Content Types:** Eye-catching visuals, engaging videos, and brand storytelling.
- **Features:** Feed posts, Instagram Stories, Reels, and IGTV.

2. Interest
- **Goal:** Generate interest in your products or services.
- **Content Types:** Educational content, product demos, customer testimonials, and behind-the-scenes content.
- **Features:** Carousel posts, Stories with interactive elements, IGTV tutorials.

3. Decision

- **Goal:** Persuade potential customers to consider your products or services.
- **Content Types:** Detailed product information, comparisons, exclusive offers, and case studies.
- **Features:** Shoppable posts, product tags, Stories with swipe-up links, Instagram Live.

4. Action
- **Goal:** Convert potential customers into buyers.
- **Content Types:** Strong CTAs, promotions, discount codes, and seamless checkout processes.
- **Features:** Instagram Shopping, bio links, Shopping ads, and retargeting ads.

Building the Sales Funnel

Stage 1: Awareness

Optimize Your Profile
- **Professional Bio:** Create a compelling bio that clearly communicates your brand's value proposition.
- **Profile Picture:** Use a high-quality logo or image that represents your brand.

- Contact Information: Include contact details to make it easy for potential customers to reach you.

Create High-Quality Content

- Engaging Visuals: Post high-resolution images and videos that grab attention.

- Consistency: Maintain a consistent posting schedule and aesthetic to build brand recognition.

- Captivating Captions: Write engaging captions that encourage interaction.

Utilize Instagram Features

- Stories: Share behind-the-scenes content, daily updates, and brand stories to build a connection with your audience.

- Reels: Create short, engaging videos that highlight your brand's personality and attract new followers.

- IGTV: Post long-form videos to provide in-depth information about your products or services.

Stage 2: Interest

Educational Content

- Tutorials: Share how-to guides and tutorials related to your products.

- Informative Posts: Create posts that educate your audience about the benefits and uses of your products.

- Customer Testimonials: Share positive reviews and testimonials from satisfied customers.

Interactive Stories

- Polls and Quizzes: Use interactive features like polls and quizzes to engage your audience and gather insights.

- Questions: Encourage your followers to ask questions and respond to them in your Stories.

Carousel Posts

- Multiple Images: Use carousel posts to provide detailed information about your products, showcase different angles, or tell a story.

- Step-by-Step Guides: Create carousel posts that offer step-by-step guides or product demonstrations.

Stage 3: Decision

Shoppable Posts and Stories

- **Product Tags:** Use Instagram's shopping features to tag products in your posts and stories, allowing followers to shop directly from your content.

- **Shopping Stickers:** Add shopping stickers to your stories to make it easy for followers to view product details and make purchases.

Detailed Product Information

- **Comparative Posts:** Share posts that compare your products with competitors, highlighting your unique selling points.

- **In-Depth Reviews:** Create detailed reviews and case studies to showcase the effectiveness of your products.

Exclusive Offers

- **Limited-Time Promotions:** Offer exclusive discounts and limited-time promotions to encourage immediate action.

- **Swipe-Up Links:** Use swipe-up links in your stories to direct followers to product pages or

special offers (available for accounts with 10k+
followers).

Stage 4: Action

Clear CTAs

- **Direct Language:** Use clear and compelling calls-
to-action (CTAs) in your posts, stories, and bio.
- **Urgency:** Create a sense of urgency with phrases
like "Shop Now," "Limited Time Offer," or "Don't
Miss Out."

Seamless Shopping Experience

- **Instagram Shopping:** Enable Instagram
Shopping to allow followers to browse and
purchase products directly from your profile.
- **Link in Bio:** Use link-in-bio tools to direct
followers to your website, product pages, or specific
landing pages.

Retargeting Ads

- **Targeted Campaigns:** Implement retargeting
campaigns to reach users who have interacted with
your content but haven't made a purchase.

- Dynamic Ads: Use dynamic ads to automatically show products based on user interests and behaviors.

Optimizing the Sales Funnel

Monitor Performance
- Instagram Insights: Use Instagram Insights to track key metrics such as engagement rates, click-through rates, and conversion rates.
- Third-Party Tools: Utilize third-party analytics tools for more detailed insights and reporting.

Adjust Strategy
- Data-Driven Decisions: Analyze performance data to make informed decisions about your content and advertising strategies.
- Continuous Improvement: Regularly review and optimize your sales funnel to improve conversion rates and overall effectiveness.

A/B Testing

- Test Variables: Conduct A/B tests on different elements of your posts, ads, and CTAs to identify what works best.

- Analyze Results: Use the results of your tests to refine your approach and maximize conversions.

Building Customer Relationships

Post-Purchase Engagement
- Thank You Messages: Send personalized thank you messages to customers who make a purchase.

- Customer Support: Provide excellent customer support through direct messages and comments to address any issues or questions.

Loyalty Programs
- Exclusive Offers: Offer exclusive discounts, early access to new products, and special promotions to loyal customers.

- Reward Programs: Implement a reward program to incentivize repeat purchases and long-term loyalty.

Continuous Feedback

- Surveys and Feedback Forms: Use surveys and feedback forms to gather customer insights and improve your products and services.

- Adapt and Improve: Continuously adapt and improve your strategies based on customer feedback and performance data.

By developing a structured sales funnel on Instagram, you can effectively guide your followers through the buyer's journey, from awareness to action. Focus on providing value at each stage, building trust, and creating a seamless shopping experience to maximize conversions and grow your business on Instagram.

Creating Compelling Calls-to-Action

A compelling call-to-action (CTA) is a critical component of any successful Instagram marketing strategy. CTAs guide your audience towards a specific action, whether it's visiting your website, making a purchase, or engaging with your content. This chapter will delve into the strategies for creating effective CTAs that drive conversions and enhance user engagement.

Understanding the Importance of CTAs

CTAs are essential because they:
- **Direct User Behavior:** Guide your audience on what to do next, reducing the chances of them getting lost or distracted.
- **Increase Engagement:** Encourage interactions, such as likes, comments, shares, or clicks.
- **Boost Conversions:** Lead followers towards actions that generate sales, sign-ups, or other business goals.

Key Elements of an Effective CTA

Clarity

- **Be Direct:** Use clear, concise language that tells users exactly what you want them to do.
- **Action-Oriented Verbs:** Start your CTA with strong action verbs like "Shop," "Buy," "Learn," "Discover," "Sign Up," or "Download."

Urgency

- **Create Urgency:** Encourage immediate action by highlighting limited-time offers, scarcity, or deadlines.
- **Phrases:** Use phrases like "Now," "Today," "Limited Time," "Hurry," or "Don't Miss Out."

Value Proposition

- **Highlight Benefits:** Explain what users will gain by taking the action, whether it's a discount, exclusive content, or a useful resource.
- **Incentives:** Offer incentives such as free shipping, discounts, or bonuses.

Placement

- **Visibility:** Ensure your CTA stands out visually. Use contrasting colors, larger fonts, or buttons to make it noticeable.
- **Strategic Positioning:** Place CTAs in high-visibility areas of your posts, stories, bio, and ads.

Crafting CTAs for Different Instagram Features

Feed Posts

- **Caption CTAs:** Include a strong CTA in the caption. Example: "Shop our latest collection – link in bio!"
- **Visual Cues:** Use arrows or text overlays on images to draw attention to the CTA.

Stories

- **Swipe-Up Links:** For accounts with 10k+ followers, use the swipe-up feature to direct users to a specific URL.
- **Interactive Stickers:** Use poll, question, or countdown stickers to engage users and prompt action.
- **Text Overlays:** Add text overlays with CTAs like "Swipe Up to Shop" or "Tap to Learn More."

Reels and IGTV

- Video CTAs: Verbally mention the CTA within the video and include it in the caption. Example: "Check out the full tutorial on our IGTV – link in bio!"

- End Screens: Add a call-to-action at the end of your video content, encouraging viewers to take the next step.

Bio

- Link in Bio: Use link-in-bio tools like Linktree or Lnk.Bio to provide multiple destinations from a single link.

- Bio Text: Incorporate a CTA in your bio text, such as "Shop our latest products – link below!"

Ads

- Ad Copy: Ensure your ad copy includes a compelling CTA that aligns with the ad's objective.

- CTA Buttons: Use Instagram's CTA buttons like "Shop Now," "Learn More," or "Sign Up" to drive immediate action.

Examples of Effective CTAs

Promotional CTAs

- "Get 20% off – Shop Now!"
- "Limited time offer – Buy Today!"
- "Exclusive access – Sign Up Now!"

Engagement CTAs

- "Double tap if you agree!"
- "Tag a friend who needs to see this!"
- "Leave a comment and let us know your thoughts!"

Educational CTAs

- "Learn more about our new product – Swipe Up!"
- "Watch the full tutorial on IGTV!"
- "Discover the benefits – Link in Bio!"

Community Building CTAs

- "Join our community – Follow us!"

- "Share your story with us – Use #OurBrand!"
- "Stay updated – Turn on post notifications!"

Best Practices for CTA Implementation

Test and Iterate

- **A/B Testing:** Experiment with different CTAs to see which ones resonate best with your audience.
- **Performance Analysis:** Monitor the performance of your CTAs through Instagram Insights and adjust accordingly.

Personalization

- **Tailor CTAs:** Customize your CTAs based on your audience segments and their preferences.
- **Speak Directly:** Use language that speaks directly to your audience's needs and desires.

Consistency

- **Brand Voice:** Maintain a consistent brand voice and style in your CTAs to build recognition and trust.

- **Regular Updates:** Keep your CTAs fresh and relevant by updating them regularly to reflect current promotions or campaigns.

Creating compelling calls-to-action is a vital aspect of driving engagement and conversions on Instagram. By understanding the key elements of effective CTAs, tailoring them to different Instagram features, and following best practices, you can guide your followers towards meaningful actions that benefit both your audience and your business. Remember to continually test and refine your CTAs to ensure they remain effective and resonate with your target audience.

Building Trust and Credibility

Trust and credibility are the cornerstones of a successful Instagram marketing strategy. Without them, even the most beautifully crafted content can fall flat. Building trust and credibility with your audience fosters loyalty, encourages engagement, and ultimately drives conversions. This chapter will explore the strategies for establishing a trustworthy and credible brand presence on Instagram.

Why Trust and Credibility Matter

Enhances Customer Loyalty
When followers trust your brand, they are more likely to become repeat customers and advocates for your business.

Increases Engagement
Trustworthy brands experience higher levels of engagement, as followers are more inclined to interact with content they believe is authentic and reliable.

Drives Conversions
Credibility reduces the perceived risk of purchasing from your brand, thereby increasing the likelihood of conversions.

Strategies for Building Trust and Credibility

1. Authentic Content

Show Behind-the-Scenes
- **Humanize Your Brand**: Share behind-the-scenes content to give your audience a glimpse into your company culture, processes, and the people behind the brand.
- **Transparency**: Be transparent about your business practices and values.

User-Generated Content
- **Customer Stories**: Share testimonials and stories from real customers using your products.
- **Reposts**: Repost user-generated content to show appreciation for your customers and to provide social proof.

2. Consistent Branding

Visual Consistency
- **Brand Aesthetic**: Maintain a consistent color scheme, style, and tone across all your posts to create a cohesive brand identity.

- **Logo and Watermarks**: Use your logo or watermark on your images and videos to reinforce brand recognition.

Voice and Messaging
- **Consistent Voice**: Develop a consistent brand voice that reflects your brand's personality and values.
- **Clear Messaging**: Ensure that your messaging is clear, consistent, and aligns with your brand values and mission.

3. Engaging with Your Audience

Prompt Responses
- **Timely Replies**: Respond to comments and direct messages promptly to show that you value your followers' input and feedback.
- **Personalization**: Personalize your interactions by addressing followers by name and acknowledging their specific comments or questions.

Active Listening

- **Feedback**: Actively seek and respond to feedback from your audience. Show that you are listening and willing to make improvements based on their suggestions.
- **Polls and Questions**: Use Instagram Stories to create polls and ask questions to engage your audience and gather insights.

4. Showcasing Expertise

Educational Content
- **Tutorials and How-Tos**: Share educational content such as tutorials, how-to guides, and tips that demonstrate your expertise in your industry.
- **Webinars and Live Sessions**: Host Instagram Live sessions or webinars to provide in-depth knowledge and interact with your audience in real-time.

Thought Leadership
- **Industry Insights**: Share your thoughts on industry trends, news, and developments to position your brand as a thought leader.

- **Guest Experts**: Collaborate with industry experts and influencers to add credibility to your brand and provide valuable insights to your audience.

5. Leveraging Reviews and Testimonials

Customer Reviews
- **Highlight Reviews**: Regularly share positive reviews and testimonials from satisfied customers to build trust and provide social proof.
- **Review Platforms**: Encourage customers to leave reviews on platforms like Google, Yelp, and Facebook, and showcase these reviews on your Instagram profile.

Influencer Partnerships
- **Authentic Endorsements**: Partner with influencers who genuinely believe in your brand and products. Authentic endorsements from trusted influencers can significantly boost your credibility.
- **Long-Term Collaborations**: Build long-term relationships with influencers to create more authentic and consistent endorsements.

6. Transparency and Integrity

Honest Communication
- **Authenticity**: Be honest and transparent in your communication. Avoid exaggerated claims and be upfront about product limitations.
- **Admit Mistakes**: If your brand makes a mistake, acknowledge it openly, apologize, and explain how you will rectify the situation.

Ethical Practices
- **Sustainability**: Highlight your brand's commitment to ethical and sustainable practices, whether it's through eco-friendly products, fair trade, or charitable initiatives.
- **Community Involvement**: Share your brand's involvement in community service or social causes to demonstrate your commitment to making a positive impact.

Measuring Trust and Credibility

Engagement Metrics

- **Comments and Shares**: Monitor the number and sentiment of comments and shares to gauge how your audience perceives your content.
- **Direct Messages**: Track the volume and nature of direct messages for insights into customer trust and engagement.

Sentiment Analysis
- **Feedback and Reviews**: Regularly analyze customer feedback and reviews to identify trends in sentiment towards your brand.
- **Social Listening**: Use social listening tools to monitor mentions of your brand and relevant keywords to understand how your audience feels about your brand.

Conversion Rates
- **Website Traffic**: Track the traffic from Instagram to your website to measure the effectiveness of your CTAs and overall trust in your brand.
- **Sales Data**: Analyze sales data to see if increased engagement and trust translate into higher conversion rates.

Building trust and credibility on Instagram requires consistent effort and a genuine approach to interacting with your audience. By focusing on authenticity, engaging with your followers, showcasing your expertise, leveraging reviews and testimonials, and maintaining transparency, you can foster a loyal community that trusts and believes in your brand. Remember, trust and credibility are earned over time, so be patient and stay committed to these principles to see long-term success.

Converting Engagement into Sales

Engagement on Instagram is a powerful indicator of interest and connection with your audience, but the ultimate goal for most businesses is to convert this engagement into tangible sales. This chapter will guide you through strategies and techniques to effectively turn your Instagram interactions into revenue, ensuring that your marketing efforts translate into business growth.

Understanding the Engagement-Sales Funnel

The Journey from Engagement to Sales

1. Awareness: Potential customers discover your brand through engaging content.

2. Interest: Followers show interest by liking, commenting, sharing, or saving your posts.

3. Consideration: Engaged followers explore your profile, visit your website, and evaluate your products or services.

4. Decision: Followers decide to make a purchase, often influenced by compelling CTAs, promotions, and seamless shopping experiences.

5. Action: Followers complete a purchase and ideally become repeat customers and brand advocates.

Strategies to Convert Engagement into Sales

1. Optimize Your Instagram Profile

Clear Value Proposition

- Bio: Clearly state what your brand offers and the value it provides. Include a strong CTA and link in bio.

- Profile Picture: Use a professional, recognizable logo or image.

Link in Bio

- Link Tools: Use link-in-bio tools like Linktree or Shorby to provide multiple links to your website, product pages, and promotions.

- Regular Updates: Keep your bio link updated with the latest promotions, new products, and relevant content.

2. Shoppable Content

Instagram Shopping

- Product Tags: Tag your products in posts and stories to enable direct purchases from your content.

- Shop Tab: Set up your Instagram Shop to provide a seamless shopping experience directly from your profile.

Shoppable Posts and Stories

- High-Quality Visuals: Use high-quality images and videos to showcase your products.

- Engaging Captions: Write captions that highlight the benefits of your products and include CTAs like "Shop Now" or "Swipe Up."

3. Compelling Calls-to-Action (CTAs)

Action-Oriented CTAs

- Clear and Direct: Use strong, clear CTAs in your captions and stories, such as "Buy Now," "Shop Today," or "Get Yours Now."

- Urgency: Create a sense of urgency with phrases like "Limited Time Offer" or "While Supplies Last."

Interactive CTAs

- Stories: Use interactive elements like polls, questions, and countdowns to engage your audience and guide them towards a purchase.

- Comments and DMs: Encourage followers to comment or message you for more information or to place an order.

4. Exclusive Offers and Promotions

Limited-Time Discounts
- **Special Promotions:** Offer exclusive discounts, promo codes, or flash sales to your Instagram followers.
- **Story Highlights:** Save these promotions in your story highlights for easy access.

Loyalty Programs
- **Rewards:** Create a loyalty program that rewards followers for repeat purchases, referrals, and engagement.
- **Exclusive Access:** Offer early access to new products or special events for your most engaged followers.

5. Influencer Collaborations

Authentic Partnerships
- **Select Influencers:** Collaborate with influencers who align with your brand values and have a genuine connection with their followers.

- Sponsored Content: Create authentic sponsored content that showcases your products in a relatable way.

Trackable Links
- Unique Links: Provide influencers with unique links or promo codes to track conversions and measure the effectiveness of the collaboration.
- Performance Analysis: Analyze the engagement and sales generated from influencer partnerships to refine your strategy.

6. Utilizing Instagram Ads

Targeted Advertising
- Audience Segmentation: Use Instagram's targeting options to reach specific segments of your audience based on demographics, interests, and behaviors.
- Ad Formats: Experiment with different ad formats such as photo ads, video ads, carousel ads, and story ads.

Retargeting Campaigns

- Retarget Engaged Users: Create retargeting campaigns for users who have previously engaged with your content but haven't made a purchase.

- Dynamic Ads: Use dynamic ads to show personalized product recommendations based on user behavior.

7. Providing Exceptional Customer Service

Responsive Communication

- Quick Replies: Respond promptly to comments and direct messages to address questions, concerns, and purchase inquiries.

- Personalization: Personalize your interactions to build a stronger connection with your followers.

Post-Purchase Support

- Follow-Up: Follow up with customers after their purchase to thank them, provide additional information, and encourage future interactions.

- Feedback and Reviews: Encourage customers to leave reviews and share their experiences on Instagram.

8. Analyzing and Optimizing

Instagram Insights

- **Engagement Metrics:** Monitor engagement metrics such as likes, comments, shares, saves, and direct messages.
- **Conversion Tracking:** Track website clicks, product views, and sales generated from Instagram.

A/B Testing

- **Test Variations:** Conduct A/B tests on different CTAs, ad creatives, captions, and promotional strategies to identify what works best.
- **Continuous Improvement:** Use the insights gained from testing to continuously optimize your content and strategies for better conversion rates.

Converting engagement into sales on Instagram requires a strategic approach that combines optimized profiles, shoppable content, compelling CTAs, exclusive offers, influencer collaborations, targeted ads, exceptional customer service, and continuous analysis and optimization. By implementing these strategies, you can effectively turn your Instagram engagement into meaningful sales and drive significant growth for your business. Remember, the key to success is to remain authentic, responsive, and committed to providing value to your audience at every stage of their journey.

Retaining Customers and Building Loyalty

Once you've successfully converted your Instagram followers into customers, the next critical step is to retain them and build loyalty. Customer retention and loyalty are vital for sustainable business growth, as loyal customers are more likely to make repeat purchases, recommend your brand to others, and engage with your content consistently. This chapter will explore strategies for retaining customers and fostering long-term loyalty on Instagram.

Why Customer Retention and Loyalty Matter

Cost-Effective Growth

- **Lower Costs:** Retaining existing customers is generally more cost-effective than acquiring new ones.
- **Increased ROI:** Loyal customers provide a higher return on investment as they tend to spend more over time.

Brand Advocacy

- **Word of Mouth:** Satisfied customers are more likely to recommend your brand to others, amplifying your reach.
- **User-Generated Content:** Loyal customers often create and share content about your brand, providing authentic endorsements.

Consistent Engagement

- **Active Community:** A loyal customer base contributes to a vibrant and engaged community on Instagram.
- **Feedback and Improvement:** Loyal customers provide valuable feedback that can help you improve your products and services.

Strategies for Retaining Customers and Building Loyalty

1. Deliver Exceptional Customer Service

Responsive Communication
- **Prompt Replies:** Respond quickly to comments, direct messages, and questions to show customers that you value their time.
- **Personal Touch:** Personalize your interactions by addressing customers by name and acknowledging their specific concerns or comments.

Proactive Engagement
- **Check-Ins:** Regularly check in with customers through direct messages or comments to see how they are enjoying your products.
- **Problem Resolution:** Address any issues or complaints promptly and effectively to maintain customer satisfaction.

2. Offer Exclusive Benefits

Loyalty Programs

- Reward Systems: Create a loyalty program that rewards customers for repeat purchases, social media engagement, and referrals.

- Tiered Rewards: Offer tiered rewards to incentivize customers to reach higher levels of engagement and spending.

Early Access and VIP Treatment

- Exclusive Access: Provide loyal customers with early access to new products, sales, and special events.

- VIP Events: Host exclusive events, such as online Q&A sessions, live product demonstrations, or virtual meet-and-greets with your team.

3. Provide Valuable Content

Educational Content

- Tutorials and Tips: Share educational content that helps customers get the most out of your products.

- Industry Insights: Provide insights into industry trends, news, and best practices that are relevant to your audience.

Entertaining Content

- **Engaging Stories:** Create engaging and entertaining content that resonates with your audience and keeps them coming back for more.

- **Interactive Features:** Use interactive features like polls, quizzes, and challenges to keep your audience engaged and entertained.

4. Encourage User-Generated Content

Customer Showcases

- **Feature Customers:** Regularly feature your customers on your Instagram feed or stories, showcasing how they use and enjoy your products.

- **Repost UGC:** Repost user-generated content that features your products, giving credit to the original creators.

Hashtag Campaigns

- **Branded Hashtags:** Create a branded hashtag and encourage customers to use it when posting about your products.

- Contests and Challenges: Host contests and challenges that encourage customers to create and share content using your products.

5. Gather and Act on Feedback

Customer Surveys
- Regular Feedback: Conduct regular surveys to gather feedback from your customers about their experiences with your products and services.
- Actionable Insights: Use the feedback to make improvements and show customers that their opinions are valued and impactful.

Direct Engagement
- Ask for Opinions: Use Instagram Stories to ask for customer opinions and suggestions on new products, features, or improvements.
- Respond to Feedback: Publicly acknowledge and respond to feedback, demonstrating that you listen and care about customer input.

6. Personalize the Customer Experience

Personalized Recommendations

- **Tailored Content:** Use insights from customer interactions and preferences to deliver personalized content and product recommendations.
- **Segmentation:** Segment your audience based on their interests, behaviors, and purchase history to provide more relevant content and offers.

Special Occasions

- **Celebrate Milestones:** Acknowledge and celebrate customer milestones, such as anniversaries of their first purchase or their birthday, with special messages or offers.
- **Thank You Notes:** Send personalized thank-you notes or messages to show appreciation for your customers' loyalty.

7. Maintain Consistent Engagement

Regular Updates

- **Stay Active:** Maintain a consistent posting schedule to keep your audience engaged and informed about your brand.

- Story Highlights: Use Instagram Story Highlights to keep important information and content easily accessible to your followers.

Engaging Campaigns

- Seasonal Campaigns: Plan and execute seasonal campaigns that align with holidays, events, or key moments in your industry.

- Interactive Content: Continuously incorporate interactive elements like live videos, Q&A sessions, and polls to keep your audience engaged.

Measuring Customer Retention and Loyalty

Key Metrics

Repeat Purchase Rate

- Definition: The percentage of customers who make a repeat purchase.

- Tracking: Monitor the repeat purchase rate to gauge customer loyalty and the effectiveness of your retention strategies.

Customer Lifetime Value (CLV)

- **Definition:** The total revenue a customer is expected to generate over the duration of their relationship with your brand.
- **Importance:** A higher CLV indicates strong customer loyalty and effective retention efforts.

Engagement Metrics
- **Comments and Shares:** Track the number and quality of comments and shares to assess engagement levels.
- **Direct Messages:** Monitor direct message interactions to understand customer satisfaction and engagement.

Feedback Analysis
- **Surveys and Reviews:** Analyze customer surveys and reviews to identify trends and areas for improvement.
- **Social Listening:** Use social listening tools to monitor mentions of your brand and understand customer sentiment.

Retaining customers and building loyalty on Instagram requires a dedicated and strategic approach. By delivering exceptional customer service, offering exclusive benefits, providing valuable content, encouraging user-generated content, gathering and acting on feedback, personalizing the customer experience, and maintaining consistent engagement, you can foster a loyal community that continues to support and advocate for your brand. Remember, loyal customers are the backbone of sustainable business growth, and investing in their satisfaction and loyalty will yield long-term benefits for your brand.

Appendix

Glossary of Key Terms

A/B Testing

A method of comparing two versions of a webpage, email, or other marketing assets to determine which one performs better. This is done by splitting the audience into two groups and presenting each group with a different version.

Call-to-Action (CTA)

A statement designed to prompt an immediate response or encourage an immediate sale. Examples include "Buy Now," "Sign Up Today," or "Learn More."

Click-Through Rate (CTR)

The percentage of people who click on a link, such as an advertisement or a call-to-action, compared to the total number of users who view the content.

Conversion Rate

The percentage of users who take a desired action, such as making a purchase or signing up for a newsletter, out of the total number of users who were exposed to a specific marketing effort.

Customer Lifetime Value (CLV)
The total revenue a business can expect from a single customer account throughout the business relationship.

Engagement Rate
A metric that measures the level of interaction that content receives from an audience. It includes likes, comments, shares, saves, and other interactions.

Influencer Marketing
A type of social media marketing that uses endorsements and product mentions from influencers—individuals who have a dedicated social following and are viewed as experts within their niche.

Instagram Insights

An analytics tool provided by Instagram that allows users to see detailed metrics about their followers and how their content is performing.

Retargeting

A form of online advertising that targets users who have previously visited a website or engaged with content but did not complete a desired action.

User-Generated Content (UGC)

Content created by customers or fans about a brand or product, often shared on social media platforms.

Useful Tools and Resources

Content Creation Tools

- **Canva:** An easy-to-use design tool that helps create visually appealing graphics for social media.
- **Adobe Spark:** A graphic design app that allows users to create social graphics, web pages, and short videos.
- **VSCO:** A photo and video editing app with a variety of filters and editing tools.

Analytics Tools

- **Instagram Insights:** Built-in analytics tool for Instagram business profiles.

- **Google Analytics:** Web analytics service that tracks and reports website traffic.

- **Hootsuite Analytics:** Provides detailed reports on social media performance across various platforms.

Scheduling Tools

- **Buffer:** A social media management tool that allows users to schedule posts across multiple social platforms.

- **Later:** A social media scheduling tool specifically designed for visual content platforms like Instagram.

- **Hootsuite:** A comprehensive social media management tool that includes scheduling, monitoring, and analytics.

Hashtag Research Tools

- **Hashtagify:** A tool for finding the most popular hashtags related to a specific keyword.

- RiteTag: Provides instant hashtag suggestions for images and texts on desktop and mobile.

- All Hashtag: Generates top, random, or live hashtags for Instagram and other social networks.

Additional Readings and References

Books

- "Jab, Jab, Jab, Right Hook" by Gary Vaynerchuk: This book provides insights into how to create content that engages customers and drives sales.

- "Building a StoryBrand" by Donald Miller: Focuses on clarifying your message so customers will listen.

- "Influencer: Building Your Personal Brand in the Age of Social Media" by Brittany Hennessy: A guide to becoming an influencer and leveraging your personal brand.

Websites

- Social Media Examiner: Offers tips, original research, and training for social media marketers.

- **HubSpot Blog:** Provides a wealth of information on social media marketing, SEO, content marketing, and more.
- **Neil Patel Blog:** Offers insights and advice on digital marketing, SEO, and social media.

Online Courses

- **Coursera:** Offers various courses on social media marketing, including Instagram marketing.
- **Udemy:** Provides a wide range of courses covering different aspects of Instagram marketing.
- **LinkedIn Learning:** Offers professional development courses, including social media and Instagram marketing strategies.

Sample Campaigns and Case Studies

Case Study 1: Glossier

Glossier, a beauty brand, has successfully used Instagram to build a strong community and convert followers into customers. By leveraging user-generated content and engaging directly with their audience, they have created a loyal customer base.

Case Study 2: Daniel Wellington

The watch company Daniel Wellington effectively used influencer marketing to boost brand awareness and drive sales. By partnering with influencers and encouraging them to share discount codes, Daniel Wellington saw a significant increase in engagement and conversions.

Case Study 3: Nike

Nike's "Just Do It" campaign on Instagram utilized powerful storytelling and emotional content to connect with their audience. By featuring athletes and everyday people overcoming challenges, Nike reinforced their brand message and drove significant engagement.

Frequently Asked Questions (FAQs)

How often should I post on Instagram?

There is no one-size-fits-all answer, but consistency is key. Many successful brands post once per day, while others find success with a few posts per week. Monitor your engagement metrics to find the optimal frequency for your audience.

What type of content performs best on Instagram?

High-quality visuals, engaging stories, user-generated content, and videos tend to perform well. Additionally, content that aligns with your brand values and resonates with your audience is more likely to succeed.

How do I measure the success of my Instagram marketing efforts?

Use Instagram Insights to track engagement metrics such as likes, comments, shares, and saves. Additionally, monitor website traffic, conversion rates, and sales data to gauge the effectiveness of your campaigns.

How can I increase my Instagram followers organically?

Post consistently, use relevant hashtags, engage with your audience, collaborate with influencers, and create high-quality, valuable content that resonates with your target audience.

What are some effective ways to use Instagram Stories for marketing?

Use Instagram Stories to showcase behind-the-scenes content, promote new products, run polls and quizzes, share user-generated content, and provide exclusive offers to your audience. Utilize interactive features to increase engagement.

Final Thoughts

This appendix provides a comprehensive set of resources, definitions, and examples to support your Instagram marketing journey. By leveraging these tools and insights, you can optimize your strategies, measure your success, and continue to grow and engage your audience effectively. Remember, the key to successful Instagram marketing is staying informed, adaptable, and consistently focused on providing value to your followers.

Glossary of Instagram Terms

Algorithm

Instagram's algorithm determines the order of posts that users see in their feed, stories, Explore page, and IGTV. It prioritizes content based on user engagement, relevance, and timeliness.

Analytics

Data that provides insights into the performance of your Instagram account, including metrics such as engagement rate, follower growth, reach, and impressions. Instagram Insights is a built-in tool that offers these analytics for business profiles.

Bio

A section in your Instagram profile where you can write a brief description about yourself or your business. It's also where you can place a clickable link, often used for directing followers to a website or landing page.

Call-to-Action (CTA)

A prompt in your content that encourages users to take a specific action, such as "Shop Now," "Swipe Up," "Click the Link in Bio," or "Comment Below."

Carousel Post

A type of Instagram post that includes multiple images or videos in a single post. Users can swipe left to view each piece of content in the carousel.

Direct Message (DM)

A private message sent directly to another Instagram user. DMs can be used for personal conversations, customer service, and influencer outreach.

Explore Page

A section of Instagram where users can discover new content based on their interests and engagement history. The Explore page features a mix of posts, stories, and videos tailored to each user.

Feed

The main Instagram page where users see posts from the accounts they follow. The feed displays content in a vertical, scrollable format.

Filter

A preset style or effect that can be applied to photos and videos on Instagram to enhance their appearance. Instagram offers a variety of filters to choose from.

Follower

An Instagram user who subscribes to your profile to see your posts and updates in their feed. Growing your follower base is a key goal for many Instagram marketers.

Hashtag

A word or phrase preceded by the # symbol, used to categorize content and make it discoverable by other users. Hashtags can increase the reach and visibility of your posts.

Highlights

A feature that allows you to save and categorize your Instagram Stories on your profile. Highlights remain on your profile indefinitely, unlike regular Stories which disappear after 24 hours.

IGTV

Instagram's long-form video platform, allowing users to upload videos up to 60 minutes long. IGTV can be accessed through the Instagram app and a standalone IGTV app.

Impressions

The total number of times your content is displayed, regardless of whether it was clicked or not. Impressions help gauge how many times users are exposed to your content.

Insights

Instagram's built-in analytics tool for business profiles, providing data on follower demographics, post performance, engagement metrics, and more.

Live

A feature that allows users to broadcast live videos to their followers. Viewers can engage in real-time by liking and commenting on the live stream.

Post

An individual piece of content shared on Instagram, which can include photos, videos, carousels, and more. Posts appear in the user's feed and on their profile grid.

Reach

The number of unique users who have seen your content. Reach is a crucial metric for understanding the size of your audience.

Stories

Photos or videos that disappear after 24 hours, appearing at the top of users' feeds. Instagram Stories offer various interactive features like polls, questions, and stickers.

Swipe Up

A feature available in Instagram Stories for accounts with over 10,000 followers or verified accounts. It allows users to add a link to their story, directing viewers to swipe up to visit the link.

Tag

A feature that allows you to mention another Instagram user in your post or comment. Tagged users receive a notification and the post appears on their profile under the "Tagged" section.

Username

The unique name chosen by a user to represent their Instagram account. Usernames are preceded by the @ symbol.

User-Generated Content (UGC)

Content created by users featuring your brand, often shared on their own profiles. UGC is valuable for authentic endorsements and increasing brand visibility.

Verification Badge

A blue checkmark that appears next to an Instagram account's name in search and on the profile. It signifies that the account is authentic and verified by Instagram.

Engagement Rate

A metric that measures the level of interaction that your content receives, including likes, comments, shares, and saves. High engagement rates indicate that your content resonates with your audience.

Useful Tools and Resources

Content Creation Tools

Canva

A user-friendly design tool that helps you create visually appealing graphics for social media. Canva offers customizable templates for Instagram posts, stories, and ads, making it easy to design professional-quality visuals even if you're not a designer.

Adobe Spark

A graphic design app that allows you to create social graphics, web pages, and short videos. Adobe Spark offers a variety of templates and customization options to help you create eye-catching content for Instagram.

VSCO

A photo and video editing app known for its wide range of filters and advanced editing tools. VSCO allows you to enhance your visuals and maintain a consistent aesthetic for your Instagram feed.

InShot

A powerful mobile app for video editing that is perfect for creating Instagram Reels and IGTV videos. InShot offers features like trimming, speed adjustment, and adding music, text, and effects.

Lightroom

Adobe Lightroom is a photo editing software that provides advanced editing tools and presets to enhance your images. It's widely used by photographers and Instagram influencers to achieve high-quality visuals.

Analytics Tools

Instagram Insights

Instagram's built-in analytics tool for business profiles. It provides detailed metrics on follower demographics, post performance, engagement, and reach, helping you understand what content resonates with your audience.

Google Analytics

A comprehensive web analytics service that tracks and reports website traffic. When integrated with your Instagram account, Google Analytics can help you measure the effectiveness of your Instagram marketing efforts in driving traffic to your website.

Hootsuite Analytics

Provides detailed reports on social media performance across various platforms, including Instagram. Hootsuite Analytics helps you track key metrics, measure ROI, and identify trends to optimize your social media strategy.

Sprout Social

A social media management and analytics tool that offers in-depth reporting on Instagram performance. Sprout Social provides insights into engagement, audience growth, and content effectiveness.

Iconosquare

An analytics and management platform for Instagram and other social networks. Iconosquare offers advanced analytics, scheduling, and content planning features to help you optimize your Instagram strategy.

Scheduling Tools

Buffer

A social media management tool that allows you to schedule posts across multiple social platforms, including Instagram. Buffer provides a straightforward interface for planning and publishing content, as well as basic analytics to track performance.

Later

A social media scheduling tool specifically designed for visual content platforms like Instagram. Later offers a drag-and-drop calendar, hashtag suggestions, and visual planning features to streamline your content creation process.

Hootsuite

A comprehensive social media management tool that includes scheduling, monitoring, and analytics.

Hootsuite allows you to plan and schedule Instagram posts, track engagement, and analyze performance.

Planoly

An Instagram planning and scheduling tool that offers a visual content calendar, hashtag management, and analytics. Planoly helps you organize and schedule your posts to maintain a consistent feed aesthetic.

Tailwind

A scheduling tool that focuses on visual content platforms like Instagram and Pinterest. Tailwind provides features like SmartSchedule, hashtag recommendations, and detailed analytics to optimize your posting strategy.

Hashtag Research Tools

Hashtagify

A tool for finding the most popular hashtags related to a specific keyword. Hashtagify helps you discover trending hashtags, analyze their popularity, and find related tags to expand your reach.

RiteTag

Provides instant hashtag suggestions for images and texts on desktop and mobile. RiteTag analyzes the hashtags in real-time and gives you feedback on their effectiveness.

All Hashtag

Generates top, random, or live hashtags for Instagram and other social networks. All Hashtag helps you find the best hashtags to increase your content's visibility and engagement.

Display Purposes

A hashtag generator tool that suggests relevant and popular hashtags based on the keywords you input. Display Purposes helps you create a balanced mix of hashtags to maximize your reach.

TagBlender

An easy-to-use hashtag generator that provides a blend of hashtags for different categories.

TagBlender helps you find the best hashtags to improve the visibility and engagement of your Instagram posts.

Additional Readings and References

Books

"Jab, Jab, Jab, Right Hook" by Gary Vaynerchuk
This book provides insights into how to create content that engages customers and drives sales. Vaynerchuk emphasizes the importance of delivering value through content before making a sales pitch.

"Building a StoryBrand" by Donald Miller
Focus on clarifying your message so customers will listen. Miller's framework helps businesses simplify their messaging and create compelling narratives that resonate with their audience.

"Influencer: Building Your Personal Brand in the Age of Social Media" by Brittany Hennessy

A guide to becoming an influencer and leveraging your personal brand. Hennessy offers practical advice on creating content, growing your audience, and monetizing your influence.

Websites

Social Media Examiner
Offers tips, original research, and training for social media marketers. The site provides articles, podcasts, and videos on the latest social media trends and strategies.

HubSpot Blog
Provides a wealth of information on social media marketing, SEO, content marketing, and more. HubSpot's blog features practical guides, industry insights, and actionable tips.

Neil Patel Blog
Offers insights and advice on digital marketing, SEO, and social media. Neil Patel's blog includes detailed articles and case studies to help you improve your marketing efforts.

Online Courses

Coursera

Offers various courses on social media marketing, including Instagram marketing. Courses are taught by industry experts and cover a range of topics from basic strategies to advanced techniques.

Udemy

Provides a wide range of courses covering different aspects of Instagram marketing. Udemy's courses include video tutorials, practical exercises, and quizzes to enhance your learning experience.

LinkedIn Learning

Offers professional development courses, including social media and Instagram marketing strategies. LinkedIn Learning provides video courses taught by industry professionals and includes certificates of completion.

Case Studies

Case Study 1: Glossier

Glossier, a beauty brand, has successfully used Instagram to build a strong community and convert followers into customers. By leveraging user-generated content and engaging directly with their audience, they have created a loyal customer base.

Case Study 2: Daniel Wellington

The watch company Daniel Wellington effectively used influencer marketing to boost brand awareness and drive sales. By partnering with influencers and encouraging them to share discount codes, Daniel Wellington saw a significant increase in engagement and conversions.

Case Study 3: Nike

Nike's "Just Do It" campaign on Instagram utilized powerful storytelling and emotional content to connect with their audience. By featuring athletes and everyday people overcoming challenges, Nike reinforced their brand message and drove significant engagement.

Frequently Asked Questions (FAQs)

How often should I post on Instagram?

There is no one-size-fits-all answer, but consistency is key. Many successful brands post once per day, while others find success with a few posts per week. Monitor your engagement metrics to find the optimal frequency for your audience.

What type of content performs best on Instagram?

High-quality visuals, engaging stories, user-generated content, and videos tend to perform well. Additionally, content that aligns with your brand values and resonates with your audience is more likely to succeed.

How do I measure the success of my Instagram marketing efforts?

Use Instagram Insights to track engagement metrics such as likes, comments, shares, and saves. Additionally, monitor website traffic, conversion rates, and sales data to gauge the effectiveness of your campaigns.

How can I increase my Instagram followers organically?

Post consistently, use relevant hashtags, engage with your audience, collaborate with influencers, and create high-quality, valuable content that resonates with your target audience.

What are some effective ways to use Instagram Stories for marketing?

Use Instagram Stories to showcase behind-the-scenes content, promote new products, run polls and quizzes, share user-generated content, and provide exclusive offers to your audience. Utilize interactive features to increase engagement.

Templates and Worksheets

Content Planning Template

Monthly Content Calendar
Month: [Insert Month]

| Date | Content Type | Post Description | Image/Video | Hashtags | Call-to-Action | Notes |

1	Photo	[Description]	[Image]	[Tags]	[CTA]	[Notes]
2	Story	[Description]	[Image/Video]	[Tags]	[CTA]	[Notes]
3	Video	[Description]	[Video]	[Tags]	[CTA]	[Notes]
4	Carousel	[Description]	[Images]	[Tags]	[CTA]	[Notes]
...	...	...	...	...	...	...

Weekly Content Schedule
Week: [Insert Week]

Day	Time	Content Type	Description	Media	Hashtags	Call-to-Action	Notes
Monday	[Time]	Photo	[Description]	[Media]	[Tags]	[CTA]	[Notes]
Tuesday	[Time]	Story	[Description]	[Media]	[Tags]	[CTA]	[Notes]

Wednesday	[Time]	Video	[Description]
[Media]	[Tags]	[CTA]	[Notes]
Thursday	[Time]	Carousel	[Description]
[Media]	[Tags]	[CTA]	[Notes]
Friday	[Time]	IGTV	[Description]
[Media]	[Tags]	[CTA]	[Notes]
Saturday	[Time]	Reels	[Description]
[Media]	[Tags]	[CTA]	[Notes]
Sunday	[Time]	Live	[Description]
[Media]	[Tags]	[CTA]	[Notes]

Hashtag Research Worksheet

Campaign/Theme: [Insert Campaign/Theme]

Primary Hashtag	Related Hashtags	Engagement Level	Notes
#PrimaryTag	#RelatedTag1, #Tag2, #Tag3	High, Medium, Low	[Notes]

Hashtag Performance Tracker

Post Date	Content Type	Hashtags Used	Impressions	Reach	Engagement Rate	Notes
[Date]	[Type]	#Tag1, #Tag2, #Tag3	[Number]	[Number]	[Rate]	[Notes]

Influencer Collaboration Template

Influencer Outreach Email Template

Subject: Collaboration Opportunity with [Your Brand Name]

Email Body:

Hi [Influencer's Name],

I hope this message finds you well. My name is [Your Name], and I am [Your Position] at [Your Brand]. We are huge fans of your work, especially your recent posts about [specific content/topic].

We are reaching out to propose a collaboration opportunity that we believe would be mutually beneficial. [Briefly describe the collaboration idea, e.g., sponsored posts, product reviews, giveaways, etc.]

Details:
- **Project:** [Project Description]
- **Timeline:** [Proposed Timeline]
-     **Compensation:**   [Details   about Payment/Products]

We believe your audience would love to learn more about [Your Brand/Product] because [reason]. We look forward to the possibility of working together.

Please let us know if you are interested, and we can discuss the details further.

Best regards,
[Your Name]
[Your Position]
[Your Contact Information]

Influencer Collaboration Agreement Template

Agreement between: [Your Brand Name] and [Influencer's Name]

Project Description:
[Brief Description of the Collaboration]

Deliverables:
- [List of Content to be Created]
- [Number of Posts/Stories]
- [Platform(s) to be Posted]

Timeline:
- [Start Date]
- [End Date]
- [Specific Deadlines]

Compensation:
- [Payment Amount]
- [Payment Method]
- [Payment Schedule]

Terms and Conditions:

- Content ownership and usage rights
- Disclosure requirements
- Performance expectations

Signatures:

[Your Name]
[Your Position]
[Your Brand Name]
[Date]

[Influencer's Name]
[Date]

Analytics and Performance Worksheet

Monthly Performance Report

Month: [Insert Month]

Metric	Goal	Actual	Notes

| Follower Growth | [Goal] | [Actual] | [Notes]
|

| Engagement Rate | [Goal] | [Actual] | [Notes]
|

| Impressions | [Goal] | [Actual] | [Notes]
|

| Reach | [Goal] | [Actual] | [Notes]
|

| Website Clicks | [Goal] | [Actual] | [Notes]
|

| Conversions | [Goal] | [Actual] | [Notes]
|

Campaign Performance Analysis

Campaign: [Insert Campaign Name]

Post Date	Content Type	Impressions	Reach	Engagement Rate	Conversions	Notes
[Date]	[Type]	[Number]	[Number]	[Rate]	[Number]	[Notes]

Customer Engagement Worksheet

Customer Feedback and Engagement Log

Date	Customer Name	Feedback/Comment	Response	Follow-Up Needed	Notes
[Date]	[Name]	[Feedback]	[Response]	Yes/No	[Notes]

Engagement Tracker

Date	Type of Engagement	Details	Outcome	Notes
[Date]	Comment/DM/Story	[Details]	[Outcome]	[Notes]

These templates and worksheets are designed to help you streamline your Instagram marketing efforts, track your performance, and manage collaborations effectively. Customize them to fit your specific needs and use them as tools to enhance your overall strategy.

Recommended Reading

Recommended Reading

Books

"Crushing It!: How Great Entrepreneurs Build Their Business and Influence—and How You Can, Too" by Gary Vaynerchuk
In this book, Gary Vaynerchuk shares strategies for leveraging social media platforms like Instagram to grow your brand and influence. He provides practical advice and real-life examples of entrepreneurs who have succeeded by mastering social media marketing.

"Instagram Power: Build Your Brand and Reach More Customers with Visual Influence" by Jason Miles
Jason Miles explores the power of Instagram as a marketing tool and offers actionable tips for building your brand and reaching more customers. The

book covers topics such as creating compelling content, growing your follower base, and maximizing engagement on the platform.

"The Art of Social Media: Power Tips for Power Users" by Guy Kawasaki and Peg Fitzpatrick
This book provides practical advice and best practices for using social media platforms effectively, including Instagram. Guy Kawasaki and Peg Fitzpatrick share insights on creating engaging content, building relationships with your audience, and optimizing your social media strategy for success.

Online Resources

HubSpot Blog
HubSpot's blog offers a wealth of information on social media marketing, content creation, and digital strategy. It features articles, guides, and case studies to help you stay informed and inspired in your Instagram marketing efforts.

Social Media Examiner

Social Media Examiner is a valuable resource for staying up-to-date on the latest trends and best practices in social media marketing. The website offers articles, podcasts, and webinars covering a wide range of topics, including Instagram marketing strategies.

Hootsuite Blog

Hootsuite's blog provides insights and tips for managing and optimizing your social media presence, including Instagram. From content creation to analytics, the blog offers practical advice to help you improve your Instagram marketing performance.

Courses and Workshops

Instagram Marketing Course on Coursera

Coursera offers various courses on Instagram marketing, taught by industry experts and leading universities. These courses cover topics such as content strategy, advertising, and analytics, providing a comprehensive understanding of how to succeed on Instagram.

Instagram Marketing Workshop on Udemy

Udemy offers workshops and tutorials on Instagram marketing for beginners and advanced users alike. These workshops cover topics such as profile optimization, hashtag strategy, and influencer collaboration, helping you enhance your skills and grow your presence on the platform.

Social Media Marketing Certification on LinkedIn Learning

LinkedIn Learning offers a certification program in social media marketing, which includes modules on Instagram marketing strategies. This program provides comprehensive training in social media management, content creation, and audience engagement, equipping you with the knowledge and skills to excel in your Instagram marketing efforts.

By exploring these recommended resources, you can deepen your understanding of Instagram marketing and discover new strategies to grow your

brand, engage your audience, and achieve your
business goals.

Conclusion

Mastering Instagram marketing is essential for businesses and individuals looking to expand their reach, engage with their audience, and drive results. Throughout this guide, we've explored various aspects of Instagram marketing, from laying the foundation with a business profile to implementing advanced strategies for growth and engagement.

We began by understanding the basics of Instagram, including setting up a business profile, defining your brand and audience, and crafting a compelling bio and profile. We then delved into content creation mastery, exploring the art of visual storytelling, creating high-quality posts and stories, and leveraging features like Reels and IGTV.

Next, we discussed building and engaging your audience, covering strategies for growing your follower base, engaging with your audience, running contests and giveaways, and collaborating with influencers. We also explored advanced marketing strategies, including Instagram advertising, utilizing Instagram Shopping, and leveraging analytics and insights to measure success.

Furthermore, we discussed turning followers into customers, exploring techniques for developing a sales funnel on Instagram, creating compelling calls-to-action, building trust and credibility, and converting engagement into sales. We also explored strategies for retaining customers and building loyalty over time.

Lastly, we provided a range of useful tools, resources, templates, and recommended reading to support your Instagram marketing journey. By leveraging these resources and implementing the strategies outlined in this guide, you can effectively grow your presence on Instagram, connect with your audience on a deeper level, and achieve your business objectives.

As you continue your Instagram marketing efforts, remember to stay informed about the latest trends and best practices, experiment with different strategies, and consistently provide value to your audience. With dedication, creativity, and a strategic approach, you can unlock the full potential of Instagram as a powerful marketing platform for your brand or personal brand.

Recap of Key Takeaways

Throughout this guide to Instagram marketing, we've covered a wealth of information to help you leverage the platform effectively for your business or personal brand.

Here's a recap of the key takeaways:

Setting Up Your Foundation

1. Business Profile: Switch to a business profile to access valuable insights and features tailored for businesses.

2. Defining Your Brand: Clearly define your brand identity, values, and target audience to ensure consistency in your messaging.

3. Crafting a Compelling Bio: Use your bio to convey your brand's personality, showcase what you do, and include a call-to-action.

Content Creation Mastery

4. Visual Storytelling: Use captivating visuals and storytelling techniques to engage your audience and convey your brand message.

5. High-Quality Content: Strive for excellence in your posts and stories, focusing on aesthetics, relevance, and authenticity.

6. Utilizing Instagram Features: Explore Instagram Reels, IGTV, and other features to diversify your content and keep your audience engaged.

Building and Engaging Your Audience

7. Growing Your Follower Base: Use strategies like hashtag optimization, collaboration, and consistent posting to attract new followers.

8. Engagement Strategies: Foster meaningful interactions with your audience through likes, comments, DMs, and story engagement.

9. Influencer Collaboration: Partner with influencers to reach new audiences, increase brand awareness, and drive engagement.

Advanced Marketing Strategies

10. Instagram Advertising: Utilize Instagram's advertising platform to target specific audiences, promote your products or services, and drive conversions.

11. Instagram Shopping: Leverage shopping features to create a seamless shopping experience for your audience and drive sales directly from the platform.

12. Analytics and Insights: Regularly monitor your Instagram Insights to track performance, identify trends, and optimize your strategy based on data.

Turning Followers into Customers

13. Developing a Sales Funnel: Guide your audience through the customer journey, from awareness to conversion, using strategic content and calls-to-action.

14. Creating Compelling Calls-to-Action: Prompt your audience to take action with clear, persuasive calls-to-action that drive engagement and conversions.

15. Building Trust and Credibility: Establish trust with your audience through authenticity, transparency, and consistent delivery of value.

Retaining Customers and Building Loyalty

16. Converting Engagement into Sales: Maximize the impact of your engagement efforts by nurturing relationships, providing excellent customer service, and delivering value consistently.

17. Retaining Customers: Foster long-term relationships with your customers by offering loyalty programs, exclusive offers, and personalized experiences.

By applying these key takeaways, you can develop a comprehensive Instagram marketing strategy that drives results, builds brand loyalty, and positions you for long-term success on the platform. Remember to stay agile, adapt to changes in the platform and your audience's preferences, and always prioritize delivering value to your followers.

The Future of Instagram Marketing

Instagram has become a powerhouse in the social media marketing landscape, and its future holds exciting possibilities for brands and marketers.

Some key trends and developments shaping the future of Instagram marketing:

1. Video Dominance

Video content is already thriving on Instagram, and it's only going to become more dominant. Short-form videos like Reels and Stories will continue to captivate users, while long-form video content on

IGTV will gain traction. Brands will need to prioritize video production and storytelling to engage their audience effectively.

2. Augmented Reality (AR)

Instagram's AR filters and effects are transforming the way users interact with content. In the future, we can expect to see more immersive AR experiences, such as virtual try-on for products, interactive games, and branded AR effects. Brands will leverage AR to create engaging and memorable experiences that drive user engagement and brand affinity.

3. E-commerce Integration

Instagram is increasingly becoming a destination for shopping, and this trend will only accelerate. With features like Instagram Shopping and in-app checkout, users can discover and purchase products seamlessly without leaving the app. Brands will need to optimize their Instagram profiles for e-commerce and leverage shopping features to drive sales.

4. Authenticity and Transparency

Authenticity and transparency will continue to be paramount in Instagram marketing. Users crave genuine connections with brands, and they expect honesty and authenticity in the content they consume. Brands that prioritize transparency, authenticity, and ethical practices will build trust and loyalty with their audience.

5. Personalization and Customization

Personalized content and tailored experiences will become increasingly important on Instagram. Brands will leverage data and insights to deliver personalized recommendations, customized messaging, and targeted advertising to users based on their interests, preferences, and behavior.

6. Micro and Nano Influencers

The era of mega influencers may give way to micro and nano influencers who have smaller but highly engaged audiences. Brands will collaborate with influencers who have a genuine connection with their followers and can authentically promote their products or services. Micro and nano influencers often offer better ROI and authenticity compared to larger influencers.

7. Social Responsibility and Sustainability

Consumers are becoming more conscious of environmental and social issues, and they expect brands to take a stand on important causes. Instagram will be a platform for brands to showcase their commitment to social responsibility, sustainability, and ethical practices. Brands that align with their audience's values and advocate for positive change will resonate with users.

8. Conversational Marketing

Conversational marketing through direct messages, chatbots, and interactive features will become more prevalent on Instagram. Brands will engage in one-on-one conversations with users, answer questions, provide customer support, and personalize the user experience through conversational interfaces.

9. Data Privacy and Regulation

As concerns about data privacy and regulation continue to grow, Instagram marketing will need to adapt to stricter regulations and user privacy expectations. Brands will need to be transparent about how they collect and use data, prioritize user privacy, and comply with relevant laws and regulations.

10. Innovation and Adaptation

Finally, the future of Instagram marketing will be characterized by innovation and adaptation. The platform is constantly evolving, introducing new features, algorithms, and trends. Brands and marketers will need to stay agile, experiment with new strategies, and adapt to changes in the Instagram landscape to stay relevant and competitive.

The future of Instagram marketing holds immense potential for brands to connect with their audience, drive engagement, and achieve their business objectives. By embracing emerging trends, prioritizing authenticity and transparency, and leveraging innovative features, brands can thrive in the ever-evolving world of Instagram marketing.

Next Steps for Your Business

Now that you have a solid understanding of Instagram marketing and its future trends, it's time to take action.

Some next steps you can consider for your business:

1. Define Your Instagram Marketing Strategy

Take the insights from this guide and develop a comprehensive Instagram marketing strategy tailored to your business goals, target audience, and brand identity. Consider your content strategy, engagement tactics, advertising budget, and measurement metrics.

2. Optimize Your Instagram Profile

Ensure that your Instagram profile is fully optimized for success. Update your bio, profile picture, and contact information to reflect your brand identity.

Use relevant keywords and hashtags to increase discoverability, and link to your website or e-commerce platform for seamless user experience.

3. Create Compelling Content
Start creating compelling content that resonates with your audience. Experiment with different formats such as photos, videos, Stories, Reels, and IGTV. Focus on authenticity, creativity, and storytelling to capture your audience's attention and drive engagement.

4. Engage with Your Audience
Build relationships with your audience by actively engaging with them on Instagram. Respond to comments, messages, and mentions promptly, and participate in conversations within your niche. Foster a sense of community and connection with your followers to build trust and loyalty.

5. Explore Advertising Opportunities
Consider investing in Instagram advertising to expand your reach and drive targeted traffic to your profile or website. Experiment with different ad

formats such as photo ads, video ads, carousel ads, and Stories ads to see what resonates best with your audience.

6. Collaborate with Influencers

Explore collaboration opportunities with influencers who align with your brand values and target audience. Partner with influencers to reach new audiences, increase brand awareness, and drive engagement. Remember to prioritize authenticity and choose influencers who genuinely resonate with your brand.

7. Measure and Analyze Performance

Regularly monitor your Instagram performance metrics using insights and analytics tools. Track key metrics such as follower growth, engagement rate, reach, website traffic, and conversion rate. Use this data to evaluate the effectiveness of your Instagram marketing efforts and make informed decisions moving forward.

8. Stay Informed and Adapt

Stay informed about the latest trends, updates, and best practices in Instagram marketing. Keep an eye on emerging features, algorithm changes, and industry news. Be prepared to adapt your strategy accordingly to stay ahead of the curve and remain competitive in the ever-evolving landscape of Instagram marketing.

By taking these next steps, you can effectively leverage Instagram as a powerful marketing tool to grow your business, connect with your audience, and achieve your objectives. Remember to stay patient, consistent, and focused on providing value to your audience, and you'll be well on your way to Instagram marketing success.

www.ingramcontent.com/pod-product-compliance
Lightning Source LLC
LaVergne TN
LVHW051433050326
832903LV00030BD/3057